A Guide to
Elegance

GENEVIEVE ANTOINE DARIAUX

A Guide to Elegance

FOR EVERY WOMAN
WHO WANTS TO BE WELL
AND PROPERLY DRESSED ON
ALL OCCASIONS

wm
WILLIAM MORROW
An Imprint of HarperCollinsPublishers

This edition was published in 2003 by HarperCollins Publishers UK.
It was first published in the United States in 1964 by Doubleday &
Company.

A GUIDE TO ELEGANCE. Copyright © 1964, 2003 by Genevieve
Antoine Dariaux. All rights reserved. Printed in the United States
of America. No part of this book may be used or reproduced in any
manner whatsoever without written permission except in the case
of brief quotations embodied in critical articles and reviews. For
information address HarperCollins Publishers Inc., 10 East 53rd Street,
New York, NY 10022.

HarperCollins books may be purchased for educational, business, or
sales promotional use. For information please write: Special Markets
Department, HarperCollins Publishers Inc., 10 East 53rd Street,
New York, NY 10022.

FIRST WILLIAM MORROW EDITION PUBLISHED 2004.

Printed on acid-free paper

Library of Congress Cataloging-in-Publication Data

Antoine Dariaux, Genevieve.
   [Voies de l'élégance. English]
   A guide to elegance: for every woman who wants to be well and
properly dressed on all occasions / by Genevieve Antoine Dariaux.
      p. cm.
   First ed.: Elegance. Garden City, N.Y.: Doubleday, 1964.
   ISBN 0-06-075734-5 (alk. paper)
    1. Women's clothing.   2. Fashion.   I. Title.

TT507.A713   2004
646.7'042—dc22   2004045910

    12 13 14 RRD 20 19

Contents

Foreword

What is Elegance?

It is a sort of harmony that rather resembles beauty, with the difference that the latter is more often a gift of nature and the former the result of art.

The origin of elegance is easily traced. It springs and develops from the habits of a civilized culture. The word comes from the Latin *eligere*, which means 'to select'.

My purpose in this book is not to deal with all the different kinds of elegance, which are numerous – such as elegance of bearing, language, decoration, and all the other phases of the art of living – but only the elegance of personal adornment and its relation to fashion. Of course, it is obvious that a truly elegant woman must be elegant in every way. A fishmonger voice or a waddling walk can ruin the effect of the most artfully composed outfit. However, the broader aspects of the subject are too vast for a single volume and, besides, overreach my own small speciality, which is fashion – and which I acquired in the following way:

From my earliest childhood, one of my principal preoccupations was to be well-dressed, a somewhat precocious ambition that was encouraged by my mother, who was extremely fashion-conscious herself. When school was over, I always preferred to accompany her to the dressmaker's rather than go to the movies to swoon over Rudolph Valentino. I adored to knit and used to make the most complicated sweaters, which I designed myself so that nobody else would appear in the classroom in the same outfit as mine. I have always loathed uniforms.

One day (by then provided not only with a husband who has always shown a great interest in the clothes I wear, but also with a daughter whom I adored dressing), I began to amuse myself by stringing together my own costume jewellery necklaces, which a friend advised me to show to Lucien Lelong, who was at that time one of the leading Paris couturiers. Carried away by the dazzling thrill of my first sale, I was soon brought back to earth by the practical details of running a business!

After very rapidly earning the professional title of *Parurière* (Accessorist) to the Haute Couture, which meant that more than half of my annual trade was with the haute couture (a term designating the important Paris designers who sell original custom-made fashions in their own salons), I also became a designer for a small knitwear firm. Everything was on quite a modest scale at first. For the jewellery, I did my own designing, selected and bought my raw materials, sold and delivered to the fashion houses all by myself.

One day I was asked to make a beach ensemble for a boutique, and that is how I first started in the couture business, gradually abandoning my jewellery and knitwear.

My own couture house, Genevieve d'Ariaux, was doing very well at the time, with a clientele of fashionable women who were kind enough to say that they adored the clothes I made, but couldn't pay the prices I should have asked. Being a fanatic about quality, I would refuse to deliver a garment unless I was entirely satisfied with it, and costs were soaring. So when Mr Robert Ricci, son of Nina and president of the business asked me to become *directress* of the salons, I accepted. I shall always be extremely grateful to Mr Ricci for permitting me to continue to satisfy my passion for fashion, liberated from all the worrisome financial cares.

I devoted my life to advising our clients and helping them to select what is most flattering. Some of them were exquisitely beautiful and really needed no assistance from me at all, for they knew exactly what they wanted. I enjoyed admiring them as one admires a work of art, but they were not the clients I cherished the most because I was of little help to them. No, the ones that I was fondest of were those who had neither the time nor the experience necessary to succeed in the art of being well-dressed, but who wished to acquire elegance by profiting from the counsel of a specialist. For these women, I willingly turned my imagination inside out in order to plan their entire wardrobe, including accessories, in view of the life they led and the circles in which they travelled.

If I may be permitted to use a high-sounding word for such a minor art, I would say that to transform a plain woman into an elegant one was, and still is, my mission in life.

Now, would you like to play a game of Pygmalion? If you will have a little confidence in me, let me share with you some practical ideas on one of the surest ways of making the most of yourself – through elegance, your own elegance.

A Guide to

Elegance

A

ACCESSORIES

The accessories worn with an outfit – gloves, hat, shoes, and handbag – are among the most important elements of an elegant appearance. A modest dress or suit can triple its face value when it is worn with an elegant hat, bag, gloves, and shoes, while a designer's original can lose much of its prestige if its accessories have been carelessly selected.

Very often a woman buys a coat or suit without realizing that its price will be doubled if, in order to accessorize it correctly, she must buy an entire new set in a colour that does not already figure in her wardrobe.

It is indispensable to own a complete set of accessories in black and, if possible, another in brown, plus a pair of beige shoes and a beige straw handbag for the summer. With this basic minimum almost every combination is attractive. I can remember how daring it was considered when Dior first combined brown and black in the same ensemble, but now this harmony is considered a classic, as is navy blue with black.

Of course, it would be ideal to have each set of accessories in two different versions: one for sport and the other dressy. And in this regard I cannot restrain myself from expressing the dismay I feel when I see a woman carry an alligator handbag with a dressy ensemble merely because she has paid an enormous sum of money for it. Alligator is strictly for sports or travel, shoes as well as bags, and this respected reptile should be permitted to retire every evening at 5 P.M.

Bright-coloured shoes are only smart when worn in the evening under electric lights with a long or short evening dress. As for white shoes, they should preferably never be seen on a city street (except, of course, for tropical cities), and in any case only in the summer-time when worn with a white dress. With pastel shades, a beige handbag and shoes are much smarter than white.

Personally speaking, aside from a plain or beaded white satin evening purse, I dislike the white handbags that some women cannot resist carrying as soon as there is a ray of sunshine. They are fine for the beach and summer resorts, but are somehow provincial-looking on a city street, even in the middle of August.

One of the best-dressed women in Paris, Madame Bricard, who was the inspiration for many of Christian Dior's outstanding creations, never carried a bag at all. Instead, she had a series of pockets concealed in the lining of her coats. But there's no need to go to that extreme!

And speaking of the little objects we carry in our handbags . . . they can be charming, even more so if they match. So decide upon a colour and a material and little by little try to acquire a complete set: wallet, change purse, comb case, key case, eyeglass case, etc. (An ideal theme for those little gifts!) The style of your compact will depend upon the depth of your wallet. But whether it is an ordinary one or a precious antique gold box, try to have a matching lipstick case and, needless to add, a clean handkerchief every morning. Personally I prefer white ones, of very fine linen, embroidered with my initials.

In short, it is necessary to give a good deal of thought to accessories and never buy anything on an impulse that does not fit into your well-established program. The saying, 'I cannot afford to buy cheaply,' was never so true. Although I am far from rich, I have bought my handbags for years from Hermès, Germaine Guerin, and Roberta. And without exception, I have ended up by giving away all the cheap little novelty bags that I found irresistible at first. The same is true of shoes and gloves.

I realize that all of this may seem rather austere, and even very expensive. But these efforts are one of the keys, one of the Open Sesames that unlock the door to elegance.

(See Handbags, Shoes)

ADAPTABILITY

How is it possible for a woman to be well-dressed at every hour of the day and in every kind of environment with a single outfit? This is one of the problems posed by modern life. The department stores offer their solution in the form of various ensembles optimistically advertised as being able to be worn 'From Noon Till Midnight'. But usually it would be more accurate to say that they can be worn from 5 P.M. till midnight, because they are almost always far too dressy for morning wear.

A simple ensemble in dark wool whose jacket conceals the top of a low-cut dress is the most adaptable outfit in this situation, on condition that you are able to make a change of accessories at the end of the day by tucking into the capacious bag you carry in the morning a little evening purse and dressier jewellery.

Patent leather and fine calfskin pumps are chic all around the clock, but the same cannot be said of suede shoes (which are fine for daytime, but unsuitable for evening), or strap sandals (which are reserved for dressy wear). All of these preparations require a certain amount of planning, and the gift of being able to adapt one's appearance to changing environments like a chameleon is not often bestowed upon scatterbrained women.

AGE

There is a saying in France, 'Elegance is the privilege of age' – and, thank heaven, it is perfectly true. A woman can be elegant until the end of her days. However, as the years pass a woman changes in type, and she must be intelligent and objective enough to recognize the fact.

It is amusing to note that a grandmother disguised as a young woman is no more ridiculous than a teenager masquerading in an outfit suitable for a worldly woman of forty.

Very young women may be excused a certain eccentricity, a sort of sporty negligence which they themselves will smile at later on. I shudder when I think of some of the beach clothes and certain hats that my poor husband must have secretly preferred not to be seen with during my younger days! But elegance can only be acquired at the price of numerous errors which are afterward recognized as such.

There are certain taboos for older ladies – or rather, for ladies who appear to be older; colours that are too vivid and styles that are too extreme, for example, a skirt that is too short.

Some shades are particularly unflattering to grey hair: generally speaking, all of the eccentric, aggressive ones such as electric blue, bright orange, shocking pink, and pea green. On the other hand, pastel colours, grey, beige, red, white, and black are usually becoming; but it is always best to wear something light at the neckline of a black dress – several strands of pearls, for example – in order to avoid the hardening effect of unrelieved black right next to the face.

Certain materials are unkind to a complexion that is no longer as smooth as a schoolgirl's: rough tweeds, bulky mohair, and shiny, stiff silks and satins.

The most loyal friends of a not-so-young woman are:

- all the pastel shades.
- all the laces, soft crepes, and sheer wools.
- necklines attractively décolleté for the evening but never strapless.
- scarves, stoles, and pashminas.
- hats with brims that shade the eyes.
- in the summer, short sleeves which are cool but do not bare the top part of the arms.

Just as light-coloured clothes are more flattering beyond a certain age, the same is true of hair. Women who do not care for grey hair or who find it unbecoming usually begin by rinsing or dyeing it back to its original colour. But after a few years, it is wise to review the question and to consider whether it might not be more flattering to reveal its natural grey or to bleach it to a lighter, softer shade. Pure white hair is almost always lovely, except when it has been given an exaggeratedly blue or purple tint.

Make-up should be softer but never abandoned entirely, which would only seem old-fashioned and ungroomed. Perhaps the most common error of the older woman is to place two bright spots of rouge on her cheeks, and I have often wondered if this isn't due more to failing eyesight than to lack of taste. The safest procedure is to (1) Use a liquid or cream rouge, which blend more smoothly than the cake variety; and (2) Examine your face in a mirror in bright day-light and with your glasses on; then ruthlessly remove any suspicion of excess make-up.

Skipping over another decade or more, let us pay our respects to the more elderly lady. And don't think for a moment that an elegant woman ceases to care about clothes after she has reached the age of seventy! There are a few simple ways of maintaining an air of elegance:

- Don't give up wearing high heels; just choose them lower and sturdier.
- If you have varicose veins, wear nylon stretch stockings in a neutral shade. They appear sheer but are really perfectly opaque.
- Select clothes that are easy to get in and out of – with button-down fronts, for example, or extra-long

zippers down the back. As you are probably less supple than you used to be, don't force yourself to struggle with a dress that must be pulled on over your head. Almost any garment can be arranged so that it can be stepped into.

– Since you probably spend more of your time sitting down, wear slightly flared skirts that 'sit well', and have all of them lined with taffeta or silk in order to avoid bagging; above all, avoid narrow straight skirts which ride up above the knees when you sit down.

– As your dresses, coats, and suits become more simple, pay more and more attention to the elegance of your accessories. The ideal wardrobe of an elderly lady should consist of a very few garments of excellent design and quality and a wide variety of extremely refined accessories.

– Wear only the prettiest pale mohair stoles and pastel cashmere cardigans that you can afford, the softest, smartest little fur neckpieces, and the most elegant pastel wool dressing gowns and housecoats.

– Finally, be increasingly fastidious about your personal grooming. An uneven hemline, run-down shoes, or an untidy hairdo are always unattractive.

In short, the evolution of a woman's elegance beyond a certain age should keep step with the evolution of her general behaviour. Both should be gradually toned down, and the 'autumn of life', as we delicately put it, should be an adagio movement whose themes are modesty and good taste. She should simply consider the passing fashions from a longer viewpoint and remain faithful to what is most becoming to her. The most elegant women are those who have discovered their personal style and who, through years of dressing themselves with care, know exactly what suits them and stick to it.

B

BARGAINS

It is seldom possible to recognize a bargain at the time
you buy it, because the true cost of a garment is not
necessarily the sum that is marked on the price tag.
In order to figure out how much it really cost you,
you would have to take this price and divide it by
the number of times you wear the article in question,
and then accord generous bonus points for the pleasure, self-confidence, and elegance it may have given
you. A dress marked down to half price and worn
only once is sheer extravagance, while a perfect little
custom-made suit costing six times as much and
worn with confidence day in and day out during eight
months a year for several years is an outstanding
bargain!

There are no handy rules to guide a woman in her
quest for bargains, but personal experience has taught

me that love at first sight is usually more successful than a marriage of reason. At any rate, each time that I have bought something because it was a sensible purchase, I have worn it very little; whereas my irresistible impulses, which seemed sheer folly at the time, have usually been amortized very rapidly.

To cite a few concrete examples, I have worn for years and years and am still wearing, in some cases:

- a beige cut-velvet handbag by Roberta, bought in Capri six years ago (it is now a little worn but irreplaceable).
- a black wool stole lined with taffeta, which I found at Balenciaga's ten years ago and still adore.
- a black taffeta coat made by Crahay in his salon in Liège, which I have worn to cocktail and dinner parties ever since.

On the other hand, I have had very little wear or pleasure out of some of my most 'sensible' purchases, such as:

- a classic black Persian lamb coat, to which annual restyling has never succeeded in giving any cheerfulness or chic.

- a set of blue fox furs, which I picked up on sale for a song, and which lay forgotten in my closet for years until I finally used them to trim the hoods of various ski parkas.
- at least 100 pairs of pretty, inexpensive shoes that hurt my feet.
- a little white mink collar that goes with nothing.
- a short evening ensemble of sky blue satin (worn twice).
- a black taffeta evening dress, to which I have invariably preferred wearing something gayer (I did actually wear it once).
- quantities of cheap handbags and countless other articles that I would rather forget. All of them had one point in common: they were bought in a spirit of practicality, without the slightest enthusiasm.

BEACH

One thing is certain about beachwear: if it becomes any skimpier than it is at the moment, the waterfront will soon resemble one vast nudist colony.

It is undeniably much more agreeable to swim and sunbathe in a minimum of clothing, but unless your figure is absolutely impeccable, unless you are under twenty-one years old and your skin is golden brown, it is preferable to wear a one-piece bathing suit, which is much more figure-flattering than the two-piece kind and much more fashionable besides.

There is no reason why a woman who is no longer young and perhaps somewhat stout or one who is merely skin and bones should deprive herself of the sun and sea. But she should at least avoid appearing on a public beach in attire that is too revealing or too extreme.

Even if you look like a goddess in a bathing suit, it is absolutely incorrect to wear it any place but on the beach. As soon as you leave the sand, you should cover it with a beach robe, a skirt, a dress, shorts, or even a rather long shirt if your legs are very pretty. Beware, however, of ultra-short shorts which reveal the lower part of the buttocks. As charming as this part of the anatomy may be in its entirety, it seems indecent when it is only partially exposed.

The bright primary colours (red, blue, yellow, and white) are fresher-looking in the sunlight than more subtle shades such as mauve, moss green, or mustard yellow, which most often seem merely muddy.

Needless to add, a beach ensemble should be completed by appropriate footwear, either linen espadrilles or flat strap sandals. This is therefore the season for taking serious steps in beautifying your feet, which have martyrized during the past eleven months. They should be smoothed with a pumice every day and softened with lotion, the nails cut short and square and covered with a bright, clear red nail polish that will harmonize with all the different colours in your summer wardrobe. Your legs should be perfectly smooth. Nothing can destroy the charm of a woman in a bathing suit more completely than careless leg grooming.

In conclusion, elegance on the beach consists of a relative degree of highly civilized nudity, surrounded by many accessories for which you have unlimited scope in which to exercise your imagination and good taste.

BUDGET

Unless, like a Hollywood starlet, you can afford to buy an entire designer's collection, it is essential to establish a definite budget and a long-range plan for your wardrobe. With careful co-ordination, good taste, and self-restraint, even a tiny budget can permit you to be surprisingly well-dressed. For example, here is an outline of a complete but basic minimum wardrobe

For the Winter:
- 1 coat in a bright colour – for example, red
- 1 matching skirt
- 1 sweater in a complementary colour – for example, beige or brown
- 1 black skirt
- 1 black sweater
- 1 silk sweater, black or white, with a pretty neckline
- 1 pair of black high-heeled pumps .
- 1 pair of flat brown shoes for the country
- 1 black leather handbag
- 1 pearl necklace

With these few items, you will be equipped for work and dates.

Spring and Summer:
- 1 lightweight wool suit, grey or navy
- 2 blouses:
  one dark
  one solid colour, but a clear, bright one, like lemon yellow, turquoise, or pink

2 skirts in the same material as the blouses; worn together, they become two-piece dresses; perfect for the summer holidays

Also for the summer vacation (if you have a good figure) you might add:

1 pair of bright-coloured trousers, and
1 pair of navy blue shorts, and
2 cotton knit tops, one of them low-cut, and both in becoming, fashionable shades
1 natural-coloured straw handbag
1 pair of linen sandals, the same colour as the trousers
1 pair of strap sandals

All of these garments can be worn for two years at least, except for the shoes, which should always be in impeccably fresh condition.

Starting from this basic minimum of elegance, with the hope of attaining the maximum (see Ideal Wardrobe), there are obviously many items to be acquired – and first of all, a good little black dress. But they can all be added little by little to the initial nucleus of your embryo wardrobe.

It is by cleverly co-ordinating each new acquisition that your ingenuity can perform miracles. A belt, a necklace or even a pair of earrings, can give last year's outfit a fresh new look while you are saving up your clothes money in order to buy a real party dress or a pair of dressy shoes.

But you must take the time and trouble to shop around for the ideal accessory and the perfect dress in a number of different stores and not be satisfied to dash out one Saturday afternoon at the height of the rush hour to buy the first article you lay your hands on. The less elastic your budget, the less you can afford to make a mistake. And so you should always keep in mind your financial limitations and realize that the purchase of an irresistibly attractive fashion fad may mean that you will have to wear tired-looking shoes for the next six months – unless you decide to go without desserts and to buy it anyway.

Alas, we can't have everything, and therefore each of us must establish our own scale of values. If, in this case, your love of clothes is stronger than your sweet tooth, I will be, as you can imagine, the first to cry, 'Bravo!' You are probably elegant even with only $21 a month to spend on clothes! At any rate, you are certainly more elegant than the woman who foolishly squanders her money without co-ordinating anything she buys.

No woman has ever lacked elegance because of an

excess of simplicity but always because of an accumulation of elaborate details or of ensembles that are badly co-ordinated or ill-adapted to the hour and the occasion.

CHIC

The essence of casual refinement, chic is a little less studied than elegance and a little more intellectual. It is an inborn quality of certain individuals, who are sometimes unaware that they possess it. Chic is only perceptible to those who have already acquired a certain degree of civilization and culture and who have in addition both the leisure time to devote to improving their appearance and the desire to be part of a particular kind of elite, which might be called the 'aristocracy of external appearance'. It is a gift of the gods and has no relationship to beauty nor to wealth. One baby in its crib may have chic, while another doesn't.

Perhaps the best way to describe this quality is by giving some examples:

The Kennedy family had chic; but the Truman family didn't.

The late Princess Diana had chic; but Princess Margaret didn't.

Marlene Dietrich and Greta Garbo had chic; but Rita Hayworth and Elizabeth Taylor, in spite of their beauty, their sumptuous clothes and jewels, did not.

In order to increase your chances of acquiring chic when it is lacking, the first requirement is to be aware of the fact that you do not possess it. You can then entrust to experienced specialists the responsibility of changing your silhouette, coiffure, make-up, gestures, and wardrobe. Know at least your general type: sporty and casual, or doll-like and exquisite. Study all the fashion magazines. Try to find in real life a woman who is a good example of the same type as you and whose chic is widely recognized; carefully analyze her manner of dress and behaviour in order to retain what can be copied. This is perhaps not an infallible formula for acquiring chic, but it is still the best I know.

Besides, if you are aware of your lack of chic, the battle is already half won, because the only really hopeless case is the woman who hasn't the faintest idea of what is chic and what is not.

COATS

Coats and capes are the garments I prefer. They can be made of any material, with the exception of fabrics completely lacking in body. Wide or narrow, full-length or shorter, there is a becoming coat style for every kind of figure:

For tall and slender women: Redingotes, reefers, double-breasted designs, box coats, trench coats, wraparounds, tubular styles, three-quarters, seven-eighths and nine-tenths as well as full-length. All kinds of necklines, including the high, round, collarless cardigan style.

For short or plump women: Single-breasted models, princess lines, loosely fitted reefers, trapeze shapes flaring out from narrow shoulders, capes, flat fur trimmings, collars cut away from the base of the neck, bracelet-length sleeves (which are more youthful for all women and increase the height of short silhouettes) – but never a full belted coat.

The smartest coats are also the simplest ones, whose elegance resides principally in the quality of the material, in the colour, and in the refinement of their basic lines. The principal designers' errors which should be scrupulously avoided by an elegant woman shopper are: seams and insets that have no functional purpose, and above all false buttonings.

From cashmere wraps to organza dusters, there is a coat for every occasion and every season. The basic minimum coat wardrobe of a well-dressed woman consists of:

- a warm winter coat with a collar, or, if the coat is collarless, a matching scarf or stole.
- a medium-weight wool coat for spring and fall and even certain cool summer nights; grey, white, or beige would be good choices, in a material that travels well.
- a raincoat.
- a silk evening coat (more chic over an evening dress than a fur coat, in my opinion, and far more elegant than a fur jacket).

Very bright-coloured coats may be worn at any hour of the day or night. But pale colours have also become very fashionable for winter wear, for example: a coral pink wool coat or a light blue one, worn with brown accessories.

A black coat is an excellent investment, but in order to be elegant it must be extremely well designed and well made.

Still, it is the bright coats which add a note of gaiety to a city scene and bring a flush of pleasure to your face when you catch a glimpse of your reflection as you pass in front of a shop window.

I wish we never had to take them off.

COCKTAILS

A cocktail party is the most typical form of contemporary entertaining. Much simpler to organize than a dinner, it requires much less imagination and liquidates social obligations to an unlimited number of people with whom you might find it difficult to carry on a conversation during an entire evening. It is a sort of unorganized receiving line, in which many women enjoy greeting all their friends and acquaintances once a year or once a month.

The perfect hostess wears a dress that is only slightly décolleté, or not at all, but of a rich material. If she has a good figure, she may even wear a very simple full-length soft wool sheath with a high neckline.

There is a tendency to confuse cocktail dresses with dinner dresses, although they are not exactly the same. The dress worn by a guest at a cocktail party should be scarcely décolleté at all.

If the cocktail party is followed by a buffet or sit-down dinner for which you have been invited to stay, the ideal outfit is a dressy ensemble consisting of a low-cut dress worn underneath a co-ordinated or matching coat.

COLOUR

It may seem safe to assume that colour is an unchanging element of elegance, and that certain colour combinations are recognized as beautiful once and for all. However, colour is no different from anything else; there is a question of mode; and a shade or combination which seems impossible to us today is quite likely to enchant us tomorrow. Who would ever have imagined that putty beige would become a classic outfit colour, that the rich greens and blues of medieval stained glass windows would be transposed onto all kinds of printed dress materials, or that, thanks to Dior, we would combine black with brown, navy with black, and even bottle green with black?

In actual practice, a woman only needs to exercise her own colour judgment in a rather limited way. Since leather gloves, shoes, and bags are most chic in neutral shades, an elegant woman possesses a selection of neutral accessories: a black handbag, a brown one, a navy one, and one of natural straw; calf shoes in black, brown, and beige. And so, where colour is concerned, all she has to worry about is selecting her hats, blouses, sweaters, scarves, and jewellery in colours which form a refined harmony with her basic garment. For those who may not feel very sure of their own taste, here are a few successful combinations:

Basic Colour Pale	*Secondary Colour*
White	Black and all the dark and bright shades
Pale beige	Black, browns, reds, greens
Pale grey	Browns, dark greens, dark grey, red
Sky blue	Browns, dark greens, raspberry, purple, beige, dark grey
Pink	Beige, purple, navy, grey
Pale yellow	Black, navy, brown, grey

Mauve	Plum, brown, navy
Pale green	Dark green, red

Basic Colour Dark	*Secondary Colour*
Black	Beige, white, toast; clear shades but not pastels such as sky blue or pink (with the exception of pale yellow, but only for a hat, worn with black shoes, bag, and gloves)
Brown	White, beige, black, orange-red, orange, dark green
Dark grey	Beige, black, all the pale and bright colours
Navy blue	White, lemon yellow, turquoise, raspberry, bright green, mauve
Dark green	Sky blue, white, beige, bright red, pale yellow
Plum	Sky blue
Dark red	Black, sky blue, beige

Basic Colour Bright	*Secondary Colour*
Blue (with violet overtones)	Black, white, bright green with a bluish cast

Turquoise (blue with greenish overtones)	White, beige, toast, navy blue
Green (bluish)	Navy, black, white
Green (yellowish)	Beige, white, toast
Golden yellow	Black, white, brown
Lemon yellow	Black, white, navy, dark green, pale pink, orange
Orange	White, lemon, black, dark green
Raspberry red	Navy, white
Bright red (vermilion)	Brown, white
Purple	Brown, white, sky blue, pink, turquoise

All of the pastel shades can be mixed together quite successfully, but only in the middle of summer or in the evening for very dressy ensembles. Pastel accessories with a city outfit often seem rather insipid.

It is very difficult to form an elegant and harmonious combination with three different colours, except when two of them are black and white.

Certain colours are more or less becoming to one's individual complexion and hair colour than others, but unless you are a flaming red-head (in which case it is usually advisable to avoid most shades of red and pink), there are no absolute taboos for the majority of women. Besides, most of them have acquired in childhood preconceived ideas as to what colours they can and cannot wear, and they sometimes deprive themselves of many highly flattering shades simply because they refuse to try them.

When you are very suntanned, it is better to avoid wearing black and navy; on the other hand, brown is often particularly becoming. It is also generally true that pastel colours are less trying for the complexion than bright shades, and women beyond a certain age are usually much more beautiful in white, sky blue, pink, pale grey and beige than in black or brown.

Red is almost always flattering and has a cheering effect on the morale as well; the same is true of sky blue, which is becoming to all kinds of complexions, all shades of hair, and all ages.

In the sunshine, you can permit yourself much more vivid colours than in the greyish setting of a city, with the exception of purple, which does not react favorably to bright sunlight. It is also wise to beware of navy blue cotton, which often seems dull or faded.

These are the colours I personally prefer: orange, lemon, turquoise, and white for the summer; black, grey, beige, navy blue, and brown for city dresses;

striking colours for coats and suits; and white for the evening.

To tell the truth, only the neutral shades are really chic for daytime dresses in the city (but coats and suits are more attractive in bright-coloured wool) even in the middle of the summer, and especially for career women.

When you are matching colours which are meant to be worn in the daytime, it is absolutely necessary to judge them in true daylight; and colours which only go out at night should be selected under electric lights. You must not forget to take with you a little sample of the material you wish to match. It is also indispensable to have decided on the hair colour and make-up you will wear when choosing a dress, instead of murmuring vaguely, 'I suppose it will look all right when I have changed my shade of lipstick . . .'

While the new colour fads enthusiastically promoted by fashion editors and department store stylists may be tempting at first, you can tire of them very quickly. In any case, it is certainly preferable to create a personal palette of your own, but without necessarily restricting yourself exclusively to blues or browns or beige. Still, before launching yourself into the adventure of an entirely new shade, you should be sure that you will be able to co-ordinate it with your existing wardrobe, even if the article in question is no more than a new pair of earrings.

In conclusion, an elegant woman must have the courage to try an unaccustomed colour from time to time, but she should select it with open eyes as well as with an open mind.

COMFORT

The idea of comfort has invaded every domain; it is one of the categorical imperatives of modern life. We can no longer bear the thought of the slightest restriction, physical or moral, and many of the details which were considered to be a mark of elegance some years ago are condemned today for reasons of comfort. Practically the only die-hards to resist are women's shoes, whose forms are still absurdly and absolutely the contrary of good sense and good comfort.

Most people like to change their way of life radically during their vacations and to transform themselves into backwoodsmen or South Sea islanders, and as a result, vacation clothes have become obligatorily comfortable or reduced to their simplest expression. Besides, it would be quite inappropriate to wear at a summer beach resort the same high-fashion ensemble that created a sensation at a cocktail party the week before. The mission of the fashion designers of tomorrow will undoubtedly be to form an alliance between comfort and elegance, and thus eliminate the danger of discouraging customers with the haute couture by creating complicated models which are incompatible with the modern daily life of women.

However, if women continue to seek comfort above all twenty-four hours a day, twelve months a year, they may eventually find that they have allowed themselves to become slaves to the trainer, Lycra from head to toe, ready meals, organized travel, functional uniformity, and general stultification. When comfort becomes an end in itself, it is the Public Enemy Number One of elegance.

COMMUTERS

If you have the good fortune to be able to escape to the country every evening from the fumes and noise of the city, your wardrobe will be somewhat different from that of the permanent city dweller.

A well-cut, classic suit will be your most faithful ally, and you should select it with the thought in mind that it should last for several years, which means that you should by all means avoid the current fashion fads. It should be as classic and as well tailored as a man's suit, and of one of the neutral shades such as grey or beige, which can be worn all year round.

If you are a daily commuter, you will need above all an excellent coat. In the summer, a lightweight overcoat or a raincoat, cut and tailored like wool, will cover up a dress which would be too light for your early morning city-bound train ride; you can always carry it on your arm when you return home in the heat of the late afternoon. A dress-and-jacket ensemble in cotton is also an excellent warm-weather formula.

If you go by car when you decide to spend the day in town, there are no problems at all for you, and you can dress exactly as if you lived in the city all the time.

(See Ideal Wardrobe, Adaptability)

D

DAUGHTERS

Little daughters are understandably the pride and joy of their mothers, but they are also very often, alas, the reflection of their mothers' inelegance. When you see a poor child all permanented, beribboned, and loaded down with a handbag, an umbrella, and earrings, or wearing crepe-soled shoes with a velvet dress, you can be certain that her mother hasn't the slightest bit of taste.

It is a serious handicap to be brought up in this way, because a child must be endowed with a very strong personality of her own in order to rid herself of the bad habits that have been inculcated during her early years. On the other hand, if a mother trains her daughter from the very beginning always to be neat and tidy, to wash her hands, to arrange her hair, and if, for example, she is permitted to sit down at the dinner table only when she is perfectly groomed, it is most unlikely that she will ever lose these excellent habits.

The more simply a little girl is dressed – sweaters and skirts in the winter, Empire-style cotton dresses in the summer – the more chic she is. The correct skirt length for children is two inches above the knee, and nothing is more vulgar than too short a skirt nor more drab than a skirt that is too long. Until the age of five or six, pastel colours are far preferable to bright ones.

When she is a little older, her school wardrobe might be based on navy blue and plaids with a navy background, worn with matching and contrasting blouses and sweaters. For parties and dressy occasions such as weddings, she might wear in the winter a black velvet dress with a wide white lace collar, white socks, and flat strap pumps of black patent leather. In the summer, she would be charming in high-waisted cotton dresses of flowered Liberty prints, and of white eyelet embroidery for party dresses. For the beach she would need a white piqué sun-bonnet, one-piece bathing suits or rompers, white sandals, and always a wool cardigan within hand's reach in the same colour as the bathing suit.

Some little faces are charming framed with long straight hair, or with a pony tail, or even a bun on top of the head. But naturally curly hair is usually prettier when it is worn short.

It is never too early to learn that discretion and simplicity are the foundations of elegance.

DINNERS

When you are invited to a dinner party, it is always a good idea to inquire as to the number of guests as well as to the degree of formality of the occasion. Usually, if it is to be a black-tie dinner, your hostess will send you a written invitation bearing the notation 'black tie' in the corner, you then will know that you are expected to dress in evening clothes, either long or short.

Dinner dresses should not, however, be confused with ball gowns, for they should be much less elaborate. The most elegant are, of course, floor-length, either with sleeves and a low-cut neckline, or sleeveless with a high neckline, and they can just as well be made of wool as of silk. Short dinner dresses require a richer material, or even beaded embroidery.

When the men are asked to wear dark business

suits, you can confidently slip into your low-cut little black crepe dress, for you can be sure that is exactly what all the other women are going to do. If this prospect seems simply too dreary (and I can understand how you feel), an evening suit of velvet or brocade in a bright colour in the winter, and of lace or a crisp lustrous silk in a pastel colour in the summer, would be quite appropriate, while a low-cut sheath of white wool or crepe is perfect during any season of the year.

As a matter of fact, a white dress in a dull fabric and of a very simple design is one of the most versatile and useful garments in the world. You will keep it for years in your wardrobe and you will welcome it like a faithful friend each time you remove it from its hanger. A white dress is just as attractive when worn under a winter coat as it is in spring and summer when it is worn alone.

DISCRETION

Discretion, a sort of refined good taste, is very often a synonym for elegance, and until 8 P.M. it should be your principal objective. But discretion should never be confused with drabness. A simple black ensemble in the latest style is discreet; while a bright red outfit in a style that was the fad five years ago, is like the stroke of an eraser which makes the wearer vanish into the misty masses of anonymity.

A discreetly dressed woman attracts a passing glance at first; but the glance returns immediately and notes that every detail of her ensemble is in perfect harmony; the drab woman, however, is forgotten in a second.

In order to attain the height of discreet elegance, which is the summit of the art of dressing, a woman must be either particularly gifted if she has not passed all her life in that atmosphere, or else she must give a great deal of thought to the question. And don't think for a moment that you will automatically reach this perfection by paying an enormous amount of money to some famous couturier! The truth is that the contrary is more often true, because a successful designer is obliged to seek striking effects by inventing a spectacular silhouette or unusual colour harmonies.

A person who has really succeeded in life no longer feels the need to attract attention, and perhaps this is why so many very wealthy and prominent women become more and more conservative in their dress.

If your means do not permit you to dress in designers' originals, you should lean even more to the side of discretion, because a garment that is not only extreme but also badly made is the height of inelegance.

DRESSES

In the morning, most smart women live in suits, and the afternoon dress has disappeared from our wardrobes to be replaced by the more youthful and less ceremonious two-piece ensemble, or even by a sweater and skirt.

But from 6 P.M. on, the dress comes into its own again, in the form of a cocktail or dinner dress. This is the moment of triumph for the famous 'little black dress,' somewhat décolleté, made of sheer wool or silk crepe, and with all of its chic concentrated in its cut and line. Later on in the evening, it is preferable to abandon black in favour of a brighter colour and a richer fabric, even an embroidered or beaded one. And finally, for formal occasions, the long evening gown may be as splendid as you wish. You should have the impression of undergoing a magical trans-formation the moment you put it on; it should make you feel like a princess. The plainest woman is always more beautiful in a long evening dress. Evening, in fact, is the only time of day when a woman has the right and even the duty to call attention to herself. That is why a long black evening gown, which has the reputation of being extremely practical, is really not sensible at all.

The dress wardrobe of an elegant woman is not necessarily very extensive. It might, for example, be composed as follows:

To wear almost all year round:
   1   white wool dress (for lunch, afternoon, and informal evenings)
   1   black crêpe dress (simple but very chic, for cocktails, dinner, and the theatre)
   1   bright dinner dress, long or short, in a rather rich wool or silk material.

Plus, in the winter:
   1   wool dress in a neutral colour selected to form an elegant ensemble with her winter coat

In the spring:

1   silk dress which forms an ensemble with her spring coat

1   pretty evening dress, short or long, in a light fabric such as white or a light colour (lemon yellow, turquoise, coral, sky blue, etc.)

And in the summer:

As many washable cotton and linen dresses as her particular activities and climate may require.

E

EARRINGS

More than any other piece of jewellery, earrings affect
the shape and aspect of a woman's face, and in particular they can give it an air of vulgarity if they are
not selected with great discretion. In this respect, it is
wise to bear in mind the following principles:

- Drop earrings are very dressy and should never be
  worn in the daytime.
- Plain gold earrings are never really elegant in the
  evening or with a dressy ensemble.
- If you are already wearing a many-stranded or chunky
  necklace, it is better not to add earrings too.

Once you realize the risk involved and proceed
with caution, you can add to your allure and even
seem to alter the proportions of your face by means of

carefully selected earrings. For example, pendant ear-rings have a slenderizing effect on full, round faces, and they also soften the hard lines of an upswept hair style, as do very large earclips. Button-type earrings add width to long, thin faces.

Whatever you do, never put on a pair of earrings every morning merely out of force of habit. Like all jewellery, they should be selected deliberately be-cause of the chic or beauty they bring to a particular ensemble.

(See Jewellery)

EXPECTING

The period during which a woman is expecting a baby is not always, it must be admitted, the most propitious one for elegance. A bad complexion, an expanding waistline, a silhouette becoming a bit awk-ward toward the end, all add up to an image that is not always a joy to contemplate in the mirror. But since almost every woman is obliged to go through it at one time or another, it is better to accept the situation with good humour and to make the most of it. Besides, some women are fortunate enough to be actually beautified by pregnancy.

Specialized maternity shops have not only placed the possibility of dressing elegantly though expectantly within the means of every purse, but have also developed new techniques in maternity wardrobes. Camouflage is now accomplished by means of tapered lines and by cutting garments on the bias, instead of relying entirely on pleats and expandable panels.

The best combination for evening wear is a slim skirt and a variety of fingertip tunic tops. Long stoles or pashminas are always flattering, but they are a blessing at this particular time because they seem to lengthen and slenderize the figure.

A good plan is to buy only a few things for your maternity wardrobe and to wear the same dresses over and over again until you are quite fed up with them. This way you can give them away afterward without the slightest regret. Above all, don't try to have them taken in at the seams after you have recovered your normal figure. The clothes you have worn throughout these long months will disgust you for the rest of your days.

There is no need to mention Baby's wardrobe, because you have probably been thinking of nothing else! Just remember when shopping for him (or her), as for yourself, not to mix together too many different colours. Pink has definitely feminine overtones; pale blue, reserved by tradition for baby boys, is really just as nice for infant daughters; and yellow seems to be a nursery favourite. But a layette based on white will probably be most practical of all, because it will permit you to use all of the baby accessories in all the colours of the rainbow which you are bound to receive as gifts.

FASHION

There are two different kinds of fashion, which might be distinguished as True Fashion and Passing Fashion.

True Fashion is a deep current that changes only every four or five years and is the inspiration of some particular creator, while Passing Fashions are ripples of no great importance, which are carried off by the winds of a single season and are invented by a number of different designers. It is the former that change the lines, volume, and length of the mode; the latter are especially concerned with details and most of all with trimmings.

Viewed from a certain distance, only True Fashion remains, for it marks an entire epoch. But it is the Passing Fashion that brings the greatest joy to the copyist, is rapidly picked up by the ready-to-wear industry, and is soon to be seen in all the smart department store windows. For this reason it is better, when you have a limited budget, to resist the temptation of the latest fashion fads, because you run the risk of being out of fashion six months later. You can quickly become tired, for example, of the newest colour rage that the textile and leather industries have decided (a year beforehand) to launch with a dazzling publicity and sales campaign. Coats, dresses, suits, shoes, and handbags will blossom forth in pink or apple-green for a season, but for one season only.

Of course, in order to be elegant, you must be in fashion. If the latest fashion happens to be exactly what suits you best, so much the better! But if you cannot bear bias-cut dresses, for example, then don't wear them. There is certain to be among the fashions of the moment a style of coat or suit you like, and you can replace your dresses when they are becoming to you again.

It seems to be true that fashion follows the law of nature by moving in a cyclical pattern. Many a 'new' mode is merely the revival or adaptation of a forgotten one.

Thanks to the astounding progress of the high

street, every year inexpensive copies of the latest designs are more chic and attractive, and it is tempting to transform one's personality with each New Look. But those fortunate women who have already established their own style and intend to preserve it should concentrate on the less startling models, which will not be dated like a bottle of wine by some current faddish detail.

One thing is absolutely certain: No woman can be elegant if she tries to combine in a single outfit the inspirations of several different designers. A fashion ensemble is not the *Reader's Digest*. At best, you will give the impression of being on your way to a fancy dress party disguised as the latest issue of *Vogue*.

FIGURES

Reduced to its simplest form, the feminine figure is either an I or an O or any one of the infinite number of intermediate stages.

There are very few fashion problems for the I's, but plenty of them for the O's.

Of course, if you are a Capital I – over 5'9", for example, and weighing no more than 120 pounds – there are a certain number of problems. But while you should refrain from wearing extremely high-heeled shoes and vertical stripes, you can indulge yourself in the pleasure of:

- long hair.
- trousers.
- narrow skirts.
- clinging sheaths.
- enormous cloaks.
- wide collars.
- big hats.

. . . in short, everything that is most eccentric among the latest styles. All you have to do is to find yourself a man your own size and you will be the happiest of women.

I might as well admit right away that I am, unfortunately, like the majority of women, exactly halfway between the I and the O. Let's say that with my five feet three inches, my 128 pounds, and hips that I prefer not to measure, I am rather like this:

And so I look rather sadly at all the clothes described above, which are, as luck would have it, the very ones I most prefer. And while I know I'm wrong, I still cannot resist:

- trousers. How can you live without them even if they are not very becoming? They should, however, not be too tight, even if this means buying one size too large and having them taken in at the waist and shortened in the legs. Worn with sweaters or overblouses which are long enough to conceal the derrière, they may not be exactly ideal for a plump figure, but they are at least presentable.
- wide coats. On condition that they are very narrow and unadorned at the top, and only flare out further down.

But I resolutely draw a line through all the rest:

- narrow skirts (it is better to wear slightly flared ones).
- wide-shouldered coats with large collars.
- horizontal stripes.
- shift dresses.
- shawls worn with short skirts.
- flat shoes worn with narrow skirts.
- tunics.
- floating chiffon dresses.

- giant prints.
- shiny satins.

The most flattering style of all for average-sized, plump women is the trapeze line with very narrow shoulders, flaring gently from underneath the bosom, softly sliding over the waistline without accentuating it, and ignoring the hips entirely. Garments cut according to this line are all obligatorily made in a material which has some body to it and holds its shape.

There is no reason to fear:

- thick wool fabrics, which are absolutely not fattening if they are neither soft nor clinging.
- bateau or high, round necklines, which give the maximum of height to the figure.
- gored and full skirts, which hide the derrière; and even pleated skirts, for the same reason.
- high Empire waistlines.

And you should simply adore:

- coats, coatdresses, and capes.
- scarves, stoles, and all vertical lines.
- long, rather full-skirted dresses.

That should take care of the shapes like mine, so let's turn our attention to the O's. Here it must be admitted that the liberty of choice is somewhat more restricted. Let's consider first of all the figures which are heavier on top than at the bottom, which could be represented like this:

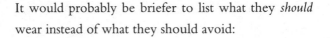

It would probably be briefer to list what they *should* wear instead of what they should avoid:

- V necklines.
- dresses which button down the front, and single-breasted coats and suits.
- draped bodices (which, like the button-front dress, tend to break up the size of the bust).
- straight skirts.
- straight coats.
- tailored suits with collar and lapels.
- crêpe and other soft materials.
- finally, if the lower part of the figure is really quite slender, trousers with unfitted blouses. The general principle is to hide what is most generous and to accentuate the slimmest part of the figure.

If, on the contrary, it is the upper part of the body that is slender, like this –

– everything becomes really much simpler, and the problem is similar to that of the average plump women (or even expectant mothers) for whom the trapeze and Empire lines are ideal.

The important point is to realize exactly what are your own physical proportions, to resist the styles which are definitely not for you, and to limit yourself to what is most becoming to your particular shape – especially when the fashion of the moment happens to be one which doesn't suit you at all. In this case, you should remain absolutely firm and remind yourself that elegance is not necessarily synonymous with fashion.

FUNERALS

A woman who attends a funeral dressed in a conspicuous manner shows proof of a total lack of good taste and good manners. Even if you are not a member of the immediate family, you should dress in black, or at least in whatever you own that is most dark and neutral, and you should wear no jewellery. During the course of a year it is unfortunately likely that you will be obliged to attend a funeral ceremony, and you should prepare for this eventuality in planning your wardrobe.

The best choice, aside from a black suit of wool in the winter and linen in the summer, is a dark grey flannel ensemble, both of them worn with a black hat, gloves, shoes, and bag.

G

GADGETS

I adore gadgets – who doesn't? – especially in the
kitchen. Where elegance is concerned, these ingeni-
ous little inventions can render many invaluable
services in the form of closet accessories, in the sewing
box, in the toilet case and overnight bag, not to forget
the various handy products for cleaning jewellery,
removing spots, and facilitating laundering and press-
ing. However, gadgets are quite out of place in an
elegant ensemble. Which means that a well-dressed
woman would never dream of succumbing to such
novelties as so-called 'purse organizers' with labelled
compartments for her personal objects; transparent
plastic raincoats, rain shoes, folding hats, and handbag
covers . . . and all the countless gadgets of tomorrow
which somebody is bound to think up to the profit of

the inventor but, alas, to the detriment of a woman's elegance. In 1964, the portable phone was not born and today there are many times when you wish it was dead!

GESTURES

Just as certain clothes can ruin a woman's appearance, there are certain traits of behaviour which destroy the effect of the most tastefully composed ensemble.

To start with the treacherous garments, you should ALWAYS AVOID:

– long, tight skirts. The sight of a mannequin precariously hopping across a fashion salon always inspires ill-concealed smiles, so just imagine the titters of your friends as they watch you move about their living rooms with cautious, mincing steps.

– sleeves so full that they sweep up everything in their path; and sleeves so narrow that it is impossible to raise your arms high enough to comb your hair or to remove your hat.

– skirts so narrow that you have to pull them up to your thighs in order to climb into a bus; and skirts that ride up when you walk as if they were activated by some strange and diabolic mechanism. (Moral: try moving about and sitting down in your clothes before you buy them.)

All of the above should be ruthlessly banished from your wardrobe if you wish to be as elegant in action as you are in repose.

Do I dare to go further and mention those unsightly gestures which immediately obliterate any image you may create of being well dressed? I'm sure that you would never forget yourself to this extent, but still . . . you have undoubtedly observed a woman demolishing her elegance by:

- diligently seeking some undesirable foreign matter by means of an exploratory finger in her mouth.
- scratching her head.
- tugging at her girdle.
- pulling up her bra straps.
- carefully examining the condition of her complexion or teeth in her compact mirror.
- biting her fingernails.
- standing or walking pigeon-toed.
- sitting with legs apart.
- combing her hair at the table.
- talking too loudly in a public place.

All of these details can annihilate a lovely impression. The charm and grace that are the foundations of elegance are made up of graceful gestures and self-controlled movements which are developed and acquired from earliest childhood.

However, it is just as unattractive to go to the opposite extreme by:

- holding yourself as stiff as a poker for fear of wrinkling your dress.
- lifting up your coat, in order to avoid sitting on it; or pulling up your skirt whenever you sit down.
- making such overly graceful gestures with your arms and hands that you resemble a Balinese dancer.
- spending your time admiring yourself in mirrors.
- playing a role, with studied gestures, perfected by practice (even though they may have seemed charming the very first time).

A complete lack of spontaneity in a woman is extremely irritating, and in the end it is just as destructive to her elegance as the undisciplined behaviour of a tomboy.

GIRLFRIENDS

It is a good rule never to go shopping for clothes with a girlfriend. Since she is often an unwitting rival as well, she will unconsciously demolish everything that suits you best. Even if she is the most loyal friend in the world, if she simply adores you, and if her only desire is for *you* to be the most beautiful, I remain just as firm in my opinion: shop alone, and turn only to specialists for guidance. Although they may not be unmercenary, at least they are not emotionally involved.

Besides, as well-intentioned as she may be, your girlfriend seldom has exactly the same figure, the same kind of life, the same social condition, the same tastes, as you. And so she sees things quite differently, and she can only see them in relation to her own taste, her own budget, her own needs. What you might choose for yourself, she sees on herself, considers that it doesn't suit her – or, on the contrary, that it suits her better than it does you – and by her comments undermines the little self-confidence you have managed to retain. You are no longer sure that you like the outfit in question; you hesitate, decide not to buy it – and yet, you really needed it!

I know from experience that it is impossible to make a really satisfying sale to two women who shop together, and I always try to arrange for them to come back another time separately.

I particularly dread these three kinds of girlfriends:

1   The one who wants to be just like you, who is struck by the same love-at-first-sight for the same dress, who excuses herself in advance by saying, 'I hope you don't mind, darling, and anyway we don't go out together very much and we can always telephone beforehand to make sure we don't wear it at the same time, etc. etc. . . .' You are furious, but don't dare show it, and you return the dress the next day.

   Or, second scene, same cast: Your friend, bighearted and generous (but seething within) says: 'Take it, darling, and anyway, it looks better on you than it does on me . . .' or 'You go out so much more than I do . . .!' (Deep sighs).

   At this point, the best thing for the salesgirl to do is to tiptoe out of sight, because neither of these women will buy anything – that is, unless you have more authority, if not more scruples in the matter of friendship, and you think that as a matter of fact it *does* look much better on you than on her. So you buy the coveted ensemble, dress, suit, or hat in question, and your unhappy friend takes her disappointment and her bad mood to another shop where she tries in vain to find exactly the same thing. But no matter what she buys, she will never be really satisfied with it, because it was what *you* have that she wanted, and nothing else.

2   The friend with a more modest budget than yours, who couldn't dream of buying the same kind of clothes as you (the truth is that she dreams of nothing else). Perhaps you think it is a real treat for her to go shopping with you. Personally, I call it mental cruelty, and I am always painfully embarrassed by the role of second fiddle that certain women reserve for their best friend. Besides, her presence is of absolutely no use to you at all, because this kind of friend always approves of everything you select, and will agree with even greater enthusiasm if it happens to be something that isn't very becoming.

3   Finally, the friend who lives for clothes and whose advice you seek. The chances are that she will be flattered to be considered a fashion expert and will actually attempt to help you with your clothes

problems. The chances are also – in fact, it is almost a certainty – that this spoiled and self-confident woman will monopolize the attention of the salesgirls, who are quick to scent a good customer. And so you find yourself forgotten by everybody, trying to decide what looks best not on you, but on your friend. Already hesitant about your own choice, you probably abandon the idea of buying what had tempted you for a moment.

Conclusion: Shop alone. And only telephone the next day to make a date with your best girlfriend.

GLASSES

It very rarely happens that glasses actually flatter a face, and if you are obliged to wear them, as so many of us are, you should choose them with the greatest discretion and good taste.

According to the shape of your face, your glasses may be slightly rectangular, round, or oval. The only way to judge which form is most becoming is to try on pair after pair while observing yourself both full-face and profile in the mirror. The lenses may be mounted on tortoise shell or metal. But it is ridiculous to give yourself a diabolic air by choosing the harlequin type, unless the upswept line is merely suggested and the size is in a normal proportion to your features.

All kinds of ornamentation should be ruthlessly rejected, especially rhinestones, cut-outs in the form of butterflies, and other such fancies, for all of them look rather cheap – even if they are made of genuine diamonds.

Neither is it very attractive to disguise yourself as a famous movie star travelling incognito by hiding your face behind enormous dark glasses. The only acceptable excuses for wearing sunglasses are that the sun is actually shining brightly, that your eyes are red from weeping or an all-night spree, or that you really have such unattractive little eyes that you absolutely insist upon concealing them. It is extremely disagreeable to talk to someone behind a closed door, and that is exactly the impression one has with somebody whose face is half hidden behind a pair of dark glasses.

GLOVES

Gloves are one of the most unobtrusive accessories. Just like leather bags and shoes, gloves are smartest in neutral shades, and the most elegant of all are made of glacé kidskin. They can be worn even in the coldest climates if they are lined with silk. Suede and antelope would be my second choice, although they are more fragile and need to be replaced more often. And finally, nylon, which are the most practical of all and even very chic if they are very well finished and if the fabric is rather thick and not at all shiny.

In any case, your gloves should fit perfectly and they should be of the proper length. Since leather glove are made in quarter sizes and fabric gloves in half sizes, both of them in various lengths, you should be able to fill your exact requirements with a little stubborn shopping.

Your gloves should also be practically devoid of trimming. With an evening gown, very long black gloves are the most elegant.

Glove etiquette is not at all as complicated as many women believe. In general, gloves should always be worn on the street but never indoors, except at the theatre, at a formal reception, or a ball. They should always be removed when eating, even if it is no more than a cocktail canapé. But a lady never takes off her gloves in order to shake hands (unless, of course, they are very soiled gardening or riding gloves) and furthermore, she never needs to apologize for keeping them on.

In conclusion, gloves are a relatively expensive accessory which require a classic style, an excellent quality, and immaculate freshness. They can add a great deal of chic to an ensemble – but they can also demolish it completely if you have had the unfortunate inspiration to buy a pair made out of crocheted lace or transparent nylon.

GROOMING

It goes without saying that it is impossible to be at the same time well dressed and badly groomed, for the two things are contradictory – even when the bad grooming consists merely of such details as a few unruly locks, a pair of soiled gloves, a run in a stocking, a run-down heel, a dusting of dandruff on the collar, or a perspiration stain.

The cornerstone of elegance might be represented

by a bar of soap. While being well scrubbed, shampooed, and brushed may not automatically lead to elegance (if it did, the most elegant women in the world would be hospital nurses), it is nevertheless a fact that a woman cannot be elegant unless she is perfectly groomed.

There is a certain kind of carelessness, a more or less studied negligence, which can in certain circumstances (on vacation, for example) be the height of chic. But these subtleties are not within the grasp of every woman, and it is far better to look as if you stepped out of a bandbox than as if you had just tumbled out of bed.

Every woman should have at her disposal a full-length mirror as well as a good magnifying hand mirror. And she should not consider herself presentable until she has checked to make sure that:

- her hands and nails are impeccable; nothing is more ill groomed (or easier to remedy) than chipped nail polish.
- her hair has been neatly arranged.
- her make-up is neat and virtually undetectable. (Tinted foundations should be well blended into the neck in order to avoid a masklike effect which stops abruptly at the chinline.)

- her shoes are clean and in good condition.
- her stocking seams are straight. (If you simply cannot keep them in line, it is better to adopt the seamless kind; and if your stockings always seem to bag at the ankles or knees, you will probably have more success with stretch nylons.)
- her skirt has been pressed if necessary in order to eliminate sitting-down creases in front and bagging at the back.
- her hemline is even all the way around.
- her lingerie shoulder straps are invisible.
- her outfit is clean and spot-free. (Some spots which do not show up under an electric light are instantly noticeable in broad daylight.)
- she has not neglected her daily use of a deodorant product, a splash of cologne or eau de toilette, and, as a finishing touch, a spray of perfume in the same scent.

You need not be discouraged by the length of this list, because all of these details can be taken in at a single glance – and a few seconds every day is a very modest investment to insure your self-confidence.

Chronic and habitual bad grooming in a woman, to the extent of really 'letting herself go', is either a matter of character or of physical or moral fatigue.

In the first case, there is very little hope of improvement. But the second requires no more than a better organization of one's daily program or a little moral encouragement in order to inspire the necessary will power to take the time to go to the hairdresser's, or to make an appointment for a manicure.

The hairdresser is a powerful antidote in cases of nervous breakdowns. A badly groomed woman is almost always depressed or disillusioned, and the idea of improving one's morale by trying a new hair style is much more than an amusing legend; it is a genuine therapeutic remedy.

H

HAIR

I hope you are not counting on me to give you the recipe for a lemon and olive oil shampoo that is just as good for serving with cold salmon as for getting rid of dandruff – because this kind of advice belongs to the realm of the scalp specialist or the Cordon Bleu. However, as far as fashion is concerned, it is certain that elegance does not stop at the hairline. It is in fact unthinkable for an elegant woman to wear an unruly or unbecoming hair style.

From a glance at the list of the Best Dressed Women in the world, it is obvious that most of these fashionable beauties have adopted a coiffure which is not very extreme to start with, and which they modify only very slightly throughout the years. The Duchess of Windsor and Princess Grace of Monaco never radically changed their hair style, and thanks to this they never seemed to age; even their old photographs do not seem dated. By following the same principle you will, of course, be deprived of the pleasure of appearing with an entirely new head each season, but you will be observing one of the basic rules of elegance, which is to discover your own best style and then to remain faithful to it.

When you are younger, you can have fun with little pigtails, long straight hair, shaggy bangs, and all the rest. But after forty you should adopt a simple hair style: either short, or pinned up in a French roll or a chignon; but never in any case long, glamorous tresses hanging down to your shoulders.

Neither should you overdo bleaching, tinting, and dyeing in order to produce some dazzling artificial hair colour. Nature has given us a complexion tone and eye colour which usually harmonize perfectly with the original shade of our hair, and in most cases we have every interest in sticking to it. Furthermore, coal black next to the face hardens the features terribly; too aggressive a red and an unnatural platinum blond are very vulgar. Finally, you should not be ashamed of your grey hair; it is often extremely becoming.

Naturally, you will make a special appointment

with your hairdresser if you are to attend an important social event in the evening. But please, don't let him build an elaborate construction on top of your head for this special occasion. Simply be as you always are – impeccable.

HANDBAGS

One of the surest ways to add distinction to a rather ordinary street ensemble is to carry an elegant handbag – and an unfailing way to downgrade a lovely outfit is to carry a shabby or cheap one. This practical accessory is so important that it merits a very thoughtful selection, and even a generous share of your clothes budget from time to time.

Generally speaking, the size of a handbag should be in proportion with your own. It is just as comical – and needless to add, inelegant – to see a tiny woman lugging about an enormous satchel, as it is to see a portly dowager clutching a tiny purse to her ample bosom.

Furthermore, the larger a handbag, the less dressy it is. The oversize models are therefore suitable only for travel and the beach; while at the other extreme, the most elegant form of evening bag is certainly a fitted *minaudière*, or fitted vanity case, which can practically fit in the palm of your hand.

Elegance in handbags is synonymous with quality, and quality, alas, is very often synonymous with expensive! However, one well-made top-quality handbag will outlive three or four cheap ones, and is therefore often a profitable investment in the end. Besides, a well-co-ordinated wardrobe requires very few handbags. I would say, a minimum of four:

1   A large bag for travel and casual wear.
2   An afternoon bag to wear with city ensembles and slightly dressy outfits. The most practical choice is undoubtedly a medium-sized bag of fine black calfskin with an attractive clasp. Suede is much more fragile, and patent leather is never really elegant as a bag. Those combining two or more colours are beautiful when carried with a monochrome outfit; but a more practical choice for a limited wardrobe would be all-black, all-beige, or all-brown.
3   An evening purse of silk, satin, or velvet. It might be either black or of the same shade as your evening coat. The ideal formula would be to own several of them, dyed to match each of your evening ensembles.

For unlimited budgets, there is a wide variety of evening bags which are more related to the jeweller's art than to the leather industry. But this area of elegance is filled with traps for women who are not armed with excellent taste. Beaded purses, for example, are only chic in solid colours, and particularly in one of the lovely iridescent shades such as blue-black, dark grey, jet black, and copper-gold. The ideal companion to a little black dinner dress is a small black bag with a gold jeweller's clasp, provided that the quality is excellent – in other words, that it is made by a real jeweller.

4   For the summer, a beige straw handbag, which can be of a rather coarse weave if you spend your summers in the country, or of a finer texture, such as Panama, if you stay in town. In any case, a straw handbag is an indispensable accessory to summery cotton and linen dresses.

The fashion in handbags changes periodically, but not nearly so often as the fashion in clothes. A design that becomes a classic, like the Hermès saddlebag, can remain in style for as long as ten years, but eccentric designs become dated more quickly. Because leather-goods designers are just as inventive as couture creators, it is impossible to predict the future. But whatever it may hold in store, it is always wise to reject exaggerated handbag shapes and faddish trimming in favour of classic forms and conservative details.

Finally, it is not enough to possess a selection of beautiful handbags; an elegant woman must also know how to choose the right one for the right occasion and the right ensemble. While it is always shocking to see a sports bag carried with a dressy outfit, it is quite possible to add formality to a simple dark dress or suit by selecting a handbag that is somewhat dressier than the ensemble.

(See Accessories)

HANDICAPS

Some women are demoralized by various physical characteristics, such as:

— *being extremely tall*

In this day and age, you must be practically a giantess in order to be considered excessively tall, because tall women are fashionable and furthermore the younger generations are sprouting higher and higher all over the world. I think that you will find ample consolation if you read the chapter on Figures. Develop the athletic, 'outdoor woman' side of your nature, and be a good sport. Everybody will seek you out for your simplicity.

— *being extremely short*

You should realize that there are many men who simply adore doll-like women, and you ought to accentuate your appealing air of 'a little bird fallen from its nest.' Be delicate, extremely meticulous in your grooming, scatter-brained, tender-hearted, and helpless. And when you are old, be an adorable little lady always cuddling herself to keep warm. Men will want to protect you throughout your life, and you will always be spared the tiresome chores which your taller sisters are expected to cope with all by themselves.

— *being born with flaming red hair and freckles*

The truth is that this colouring is particularly attractive, and it is therefore more of an advantage than a handicap. The only negative point is that you may be deprived of the pleasure of wearing certain shades of red and pink and of sunbathing for any length of time. Of course, if you simply detest the colour of your hair, you can always dye it to another shade.

– a heavy bust

An oversized bosom is indeed a real handicap in wearing the modern fashions. If you cannot stand the sight of yourself in a sweater, wear over it an un-buttoned vest, which will tend to cut the width of the bustline, just as scarves and stoles will do. If your top-heaviness is really a nightmare to you, save up your money for a plastic surgery operation. Personally, if I had to choose between operating on an unattractive nose and an overdeveloped bosom, I would correct the latter without the slightest hesitation.

If you have a twin sister, for heaven's sake, as soon as you are old enough to buy your own clothes, never, never choose the same as she does!

Finally, many women develop complexes over supposed defects, which exist only in their imagination. When I hear a woman complain during a dress fitting that her hips are much too thin, for example, I sometimes regret that I cannot trade her mine for hers. She would soon find out how her hip problems would multiply!

Even if nature has been rather stingy with you in its gifts, it is useless to moan about what you haven't got. Instead, exercise your ingenuity in playing up your best features and in camouflaging the rest.

Elegance is also a matter of good humour and of optimism.

HEMS

While hemlines go up and down obediently according to the caprices of their masters, the fashion designers, there are nevertheless a few basic principles which remain invariable:

- straight skirts should be one inch longer than full ones.
- hemlines should be half an inch lower in the back than in the front.
- your full-length coats should be one half to one inch longer than all of your skirts and dresses; and your slips and petticoats one and a half to two inches shorter than your dresses.
- the height of your heels affects the height of your

hemline, and a skirt to be worn with flat shoes should be slightly shorter than skirts with which you wear high heels.

The manner in which a hem is sewn sometimes proclaims more loudly than a label the price you have paid for a garment, and it is often worthwhile to undo the machine-stitched hem of a ready-made dress and to sew it properly before you wear it for the first time.

The standard depth of a hem is two inches, and the stitches should be completely invisible from the exterior. Whenever possible, they are concealed in the thickness of the fabric or, if the material is extremely fine, the skirt should be lined and the hem stitched to the lining. When the material is transparent, there is no hem at all and the edge is finished by hand-rolling, like a handkerchief. Tulle is never hemmed either, but merely cut off neatly at the proper length.

Fabrics which are apt to unravel, such as coarse tweeds, jersey, and knitting, should have their edges entirely overstitched before hemming. The cut edge of scratchy materials should be finished with a narrow ribbon which is sewn over the cut edge; the hem is then stitched through the ribbon.

One of the secrets of the haute couture is to baste a bias strip of flannel inside the fold of the hem so that the lower edge of the garment will be slightly rounded and not flattened into a sharp crease when it comes back from the cleaner.

HUSBANDS (AND BEAUX)

There are three kinds of husbands:

1   *The Blind Man*, who says, 'Isn't that a new suit, darling?' when he at last notices the ensemble you have been wearing for the past two years. There really isn't any point in discussing him, so let's leave him in peace. At least he has one advantage: he lets you dress as you please.

2   *The Ideal Husband*, who notices everything, is genuinely interested in your clothes, makes suggestions, understands fashion, appreciates it, enjoys discussing it, knows just what suits you best and what you need, and admires you more than all the other women in the world. If you possess this dream man, hang on to him. He is extremely rare.

3   *The Dictator*, who knows far better than you what is becoming to you and who decides if the current

styles are good or not and which shop or dressmaker you ought to go to. This type of man's ideas on fashion are sometimes up to date, but most often he has been so impressed by the way his mother used to dress that his taste is, to say the least, about twenty years behind the times.

I am not a psychologist, but I am convinced that this state of affairs can lead to disastrous complexes of timidity and dissatisfaction. To improve one's physical appearance is, after all, one of the essential feminine activities, and the men who wish to invade this realm and to reign over it like despots run the risk of stifling all sense of initiative in their wives . . . even in quite different domains.

Nevertheless, there are always more husbands than you might imagine who accompany their wives to help them select their wardrobes. They usually know just what they like, have a rather conservative taste and very definite ideas of their own, especially where colour is concerned. But they are always more vulnerable to the persuasive argument of the sales-girl, and in the end are always more extravagant than women.

I often wonder if they sacrifice their precious time

in order to avoid expensive errors, or out of a sincere concern for their wives' elegance. The wives always seem to be extremely flattered by the interest they inspire and the trouble that is taken over them. But my personal reaction would be one of considerable annoyance at the lack of confidence shown in my own taste.

I

IDEAL WARDROBE

FOR AN ELEGANT WOMAN

WINTER

 9 A.M. Tweed skirts in the brown autumn shades and harmonizing sweaters (the British are peerless in this realm), worn under a good coat, well cut. Brown shoes with medium heels and a capacious brown alligator bag. (A really elegant woman never wears black in the morning.)

1 P.M. A wool suit in a solid colour (neither brown nor black). Underneath the jacket, a harmonizing sweater, jersey blouse, or

sleeveless dress. An ensemble consisting of a suit and matching cape or pashmina is also very practical and as warm as toast.

3 P.M. A wool dress in a becoming shade that matches or contrasts with:

A pretty town coat in a vivid colour. (If you can only buy one thing from a quality shop or name designer make yourself a present of a really superb, bright-coloured wool coat. Fortunately, it is one of the easiest garments to buy in a sale.)

6 P.M. A black wool dress, not very décolleté. This is the triumph of the haute couture and the uniform of city dwellers. It will take you everywhere, from the bistro to the theatre, stopping en route for all the informal dinner parties on your social calendar.

7 P.M. A black crêpe dress, this one quite décolleté, for more formal dinners and more elegant restaurants.

8 P.M. A matching coat and dress that is called a 'cocktail ensemble' in Paris, but in reality is often far too dressy for such an occasion, although perfect for theatre openings and very elegant black-tie dinner parties. If it is in silk, velvet, or coloured brocade, you should plan on having a second dress that goes with the same coat, a little dressier still, for entertaining at home.

10 P.M. A long formal evening dress that can be worn all year round (which means that you should avoid velvet and black). And, if you are really mad about clothes and prepared to make the necessary sacrifices . . .

A long evening coat, the most luxurious garment in a wardrobe and, strange as it seems, even quite a sensible acquisition if you manage to pick it up in a sale.

9 A.M. A tailored tweed suit, Chanel-type, in a soft, delicate shade. Matching blouse.

1 P.M. A smooth, lightweight wool suit in a solid colour, a little dressier than the first one.

A linen suit for very warm weather.

(These three ensembles can be worn from one year to the next and need only be renewed about once every three years.)

A lightweight wool coat which will be just as attractive in the autumn, and for this reason you should resist the natural springtime temptation of navy blue. Personally, I prefer grey flannel, red, green, white, and beige, all of which can be worn practically all year round. A matching skirt.

6 P.M. A dress or two-piece ensemble in navy or black silk, to be worn alone with a wide straw hat to cocktail parties. This ensemble might also be made of printed silk, but it is very difficult to find a really lovely print. Whatever you select, the same outfit is perfect for outdoor dining.

 8 P.M. An ensemble for First Nights and black-tie dinners just like the winter ones – perhaps even the very same; a beaded dress, for example, can be worn all year round, and your black crêpe will be very chic in the springtime worn under a white coat.

SUMMER IN THE CITY

Light, cool dresses in cotton or linen for the morning, and in silk for the afternoon and evening, all of them preferably sleeveless and owing their elegance more to colour than to a complicated cut. These frocks are the outstanding achievement of the ready-to-wear industry.

J

JEWELLERY

Jewellery is the only element of an ensemble whose sole purpose is elegance, and elegance in jewellery is a highly individual matter. It is therefore impossible to say that only a particular kind of jewellery should be worn in order to personalize or to add distinction to a particular type of outfit. One thing however is certain: an elegant woman, even if she adores jewellery as much as I do, should never indulge her fancy to the point of resembling a Christmas tree dripping with ornaments.

During the daytime, you can wear at the very most a ring on each hand (on the ring finger or the little finger, never on the others, and with a wedding and engagement ring counting as one), a wrist watch, a string of pearls or beads, and, if your dress is perfectly simple and unadorned, a pin or clip. You can always wear a clip on the collar or shoulder of a coat or suit, but if you wear a necklace it should be worn inside rather than over the jacket and should only be visible at the neckline.

If you are already wearing a pin, a ring, a watch, and a necklace, it is better to refrain from adding a pair of earrings too, unless they are very simple clips rather than the pendant type. Moreover, it is not often a good idea to wear drop earrings at the same time as a necklace, because the combination draws all the attention to the lower part of your face, which it thus has a tendency to widen and shorten. For the same reason, it is usually more becoming to place a clip or pin rather far away from the face, when you are already wearing a necklace and earrings.

Chunky gold bracelets with handsome baubles or charms of semiprecious stones are amusing and chic, provided that you remove all your other jewellery.

In the evening, if you are wearing a dressy ensemble, your wrist watch should be tucked away in your top bureau drawer until the following morning, unless it is concealed in a diamond bracelet – which is no longer particularly fashionable. And need I add that rings or bracelets should never be worn over long evening gloves? Even though some very prominent queens and princesses may regularly break this rule, it only proves that royal protocol is not always compatible with elegance.

Generally speaking, plain gold jewellery is not very elegant in the evening, and you should never wear gold at the same time as gems in platinum settings. Some perfectly beautiful jewellery is made of precious stones set in gold – a combination of turquoise, sapphire, and gold, for example, or gold set pearls combined with diamonds and emeralds – but these cannot be worn at the same time as jewellery set in platinum.

A very formal evening dress, if it is neither embroidered nor beaded, can carry off a clip, necklace, earrings, rings and bracelets, and even a tiara, if everything matches.

If they have been acquired over a very long period of time, it may be necessary to have the earliest gifts reset, since most jewellery (with the exception of solitaire rings and pearls) goes out of fashion every twenty years or so. On the other hand, if you have been fortunate enough to inherit the collection of your great-grandmother, it has, like antique furniture, acquired considerable chic and value, and you can wear these jewels in their original form with the greatest of pleasure and elegance.

In those days, certain stones, such as amethysts, cornelians, topazes, cameos, peridots, etc., were used much more often than they are today; perhaps that is why these gems are most chic when they are mounted in an antique setting. An exception should be made for zircons, however. These glittering stones, which were often used in the Victorian era as a substitute for diamond brilliants, may be classified as 'imitations,' and for this reason they do not really belong in an elegant jewellery wardrobe.

One particularly perplexing jewellery problem is travel. It is obviously imprudent as well as immodest to flaunt an impressive display of jewellery when you are travelling. Besides, the velvet case at the bottom of a woman's handbag is the dream of every thief and the nightmare of all insurance men after a heavy meal. It is advisable to take with you on a trip only a minimum amount of real jewellery, and to deposit the rest of your treasures in a safe-deposit box at the bank. But if the purpose of your trip is to spend a week in the country, there should be no cause for anxiety, because in the country it is good taste to wear no jewellery at all.

The price and size of a gem is not always a measure of its beauty, except in the case of a solitaire or a string of pearls. A simple jewel set in an exquisite and original manner – is far more elegant than a cluster of enormous diamonds assembled in prosaic fashion merely to create an impression of wealth.

Combinations of stones are very fashionable, and the most chic in my opinion are white and yellow diamonds, sapphires and emeralds, and turquoise and diamonds. In a less formal style, coral is a marvellous element that combines beautifully with many other precious materials, such as pearls, white jade, turquoise, and even with diamonds.

With jewellers, there are many advantages in dealing with the very best. Even though you may pay 20 per cent more, you must admit that to open a velvet case from Cartier, Van Cleef & Arpels, or Tiffany gives you 20 per cent more of a thrill than to receive a gift box from a high street jewellery shop. And then too, a busy and bewildered husband has a far greater chance of making a tasteful choice.

An engagement ring is often the only real jewel that a woman owns. Therefore, to be brutally frank, it should not be too, too modest in size – let's say, not less than three carats – because a baby diamond drowned in a sea of platinum is very touching but at the same time a bit pathetic. It is infinitely smarter and less likely to ruin a young husband at the very outset of married life to select an engagement ring paved with tiny brilliants and sapphires, for example, but beautifully designed and of respectable size. Another formula is to eliminate the conventional engagement ring entirely and to invest one's savings in a wedding band of baguette diamonds. The proud and happy bride can then satisfy her craving for gems by buying . . .

Costume Jewellery. First of all, an excellent necklace of cultured or imitation pearls – and that is all as far as 'imitation' jewellery is concerned. Nothing is less chic, more unattractive and comparatively ruinous, than an imitation jewel attempting to pass itself off for the real thing. It belongs in the same category as the nylon coat masquerading as mink, both of them an unpardonable offence against elegance.

But costume jewellery that is not ashamed to be itself is often very charming as well as very chic, and it can add a note of great elegance to an ensemble. Designers present a new collection of outfit jewellery each season, and some of the richest women in the world enjoy buying and wearing these 'fantasy' gems.

The necklaces (particularly bright-coloured or all-white beads for summer wear), earrings, and clips enjoy the greatest success; the bracelets somewhat less; and the rings none at all.

This kind of jewellery should, of course, be selected with care, and, as a general rule, only one important piece should be worn at a time. All of these ornaments have the advantage of being ephemeral; they can be selected especially to complete a particular outfit; they can travel without causing palpitations and even bring new charm or an exotic note to a woman's appearance. They should, however, be reserved for feminine and sophisticated women, since the tweedy, outdoor type is seldom able to carry them off with the necessary flair.

There is just one piece of jewellery that is equally becoming to everybody, lovely with almost every ensemble, appropriate for almost every occasion, and indispensable in every woman's wardrobe . . . long live the pearl necklace, true or false, from our first date until our last breath!

(See Necklaces, Earrings, Rings)

JOBS

The women who has a job also has more clothes problems than the woman who stays at home, for she must appear fresh, clean, neat, and well-pressed from morning until night.

If she is an office worker, her ideal working outfit is a wool skirt, worn with a fine wool sweater in the winter and a shirt in the summer. Only one thing can destroy the charm of this simple outfit: a provocative brassière.

Women whose career is in journalism or fashion owe it to themselves to make a special effort to present a particularly refined appearance. This may seem to be an obvious remark, but I wish that you could see how few well-dressed women there are at a fashion showing for the press. It makes me wonder sometimes . . . especially when you realize that these are the women who can make and unmake the reputation of a designer by their newspaper and magazine articles.

The ideal basic outfit for a career woman is a wool suit or a coat and matching skirt, worn with a harmonizing sweater or blouse in a subtle tone. If you don't like sweaters (but who doesn't like them?) a two-piece ensemble is preferable to a dress, which often seems slightly overdressed in an office, requires an excellent design and fit, and permits less freedom of movement.

Generally speaking, a career woman should avoid all frilly trimmings, printed materials, aggressive colours, shaggy woollens, very lightweight fabrics that are certain to wrinkle, skirts that are too short, too full, or too narrow – in short, everything that might seem vulgar or extreme.

During working hours even more than at any other time, it is good taste to adopt a policy of restraint and moderation.

(See Adaptability)

K

KNEES

The proverb: *Pour vivre heureux, vivons cachés** was invented for them!

*'To stay happy, stay hidden.'

L

LEATHER

Leather garments should be primarily practical, for while they are perfectly adapted to a very casual kind of life, they are never really elegant in town.

If you have a real passion for leather, try to satisfy your craving with a hip-length suede jacket, or with a shiny leather coat that can double as a raincoat and will be useful in many ways on weekends, in convertible cars, and during country hikes. But don't involve yourself in the purchase of a skirt or trousers which will surely start to bag at the end of a few days, no matter how slim-hipped you are.

LINGERIE

The number of articles of lingerie worn by a fashionable woman has considerably diminished since the early twentieth century. She started out equipped with a brassière, a chemise, a corset, a pair of underpants and a slip, but today she has reached the point where she wears only pants and a bra.

A woman's age and social position are not of the slightest influence in this particular field. In fact, it is often the most elegantly and expensively attired women who wear the least underclothes, for all of their dresses are lined with silk and many of their gowns have built-in bras. And yet there exist in every price range perfectly charming lingerie ensembles in bright or pastel colours and even in prints, which would make their undressed appearance much more attractive.

Women are making a mistake in neglecting this potential added attraction to their charms. Although I certainly do not advise going so far as to indulge in the seductive lingerie styles more suitable for strip-tease, it is still to a woman's advantage to give as much thought to undressing as she does to dressing. (I am reminded of a friend to whom I once confided how worried I was because my teen-age daughter was completely disinterested in pretty lingerie. Her reply was that I shouldn't really worry until the day she did start to take an interest in it!)

Marvellous progress has been made in foundation garments in recent years. No more tortuous whalebones, no more hot rubber materials hugging you affectionately around the waist. The miracle fibres such as Lycra and nylon hold your curves with just as much devotion but without the same inconveniences.

Even though a woman's lingerie may be reduced to two pieces, they should at least be matching. It is the height of negligence to wear a white brassière with black pants or the reverse. Bright-coloured undergarments are charming, but of course they can only be worn under dresses which are opaque or dark. In the summer, it is preferable to stick to white.

LUGGAGE

Your various pieces of luggage are useful servants, but they are very indiscreet ones, for they reveal your social situation even more clearly than does your attire. They also reveal, according to the way in which they are packed, your character and habits; and I for one would not hold a very high opinion of the woman who carelessly throws her shoes on top of her nightdresses, for example, without taking the precaution of enveloping them in special shoe bags.

From the briefcase stuffed with papers, a tooth-brush, and a razor, carried by a busy executive on a lightning business trip, to the mountain of strictly matching white leather bags carried by a crew of porters in the wake of a famous movie star who drips with mink and clutches to her bosom an alligator jewel case, there exists a wide range of more or less elegant luggage. It is rather rare, except in the above case of the film celebrity, to buy an entire set of matching luggage at one time. Moreover, a complete series of obviously brand-new bags always seems somewhat *nouveau riche*, except when they accompany a newlywed couple on their honeymoon. It is smarter and less onerous as well to buy one or two pieces at a time, according to your needs, if not of the identical design, at least of the same colour scheme-beige and tan, for example, or all black. Patterned bags should be either all of the same colour and style, or else combined with solid-coloured luggage of the same leather as the reinforcements on the patterned pieces.

The feminine toilet case has been very much simplified over the years and considerably reduced in volume and in weight. Today the most elegant are the fitted or unfitted rectangular cases in which a woman can place her jars and bottles right side up. Personally, I consider it unnecessary to encumber myself with this additional piece of luggage, and I prefer a large, waterproof plastic pouch, filled with little plastic containers for my different lotions and creams.

Nowadays there is not much point in travelling with a great quantity and variety of beauty products, unless you are setting forth on a very long journey to a primitive land that has not yet been discovered by Elizabeth Arden. It is better to fill your plastic containers with no more than the amount necessary for the duration of your voyage.

When packing a suitcase, you should stow your belongings in the following order: first of all, at the bottom, heavy articles such as shoes, toilet articles, and handbags; next, everything that is unlikely to wrinkle – lingerie, sweaters, and trousers – arranging them in such a way that you will end up with a flat, even surface on which you can then smoothly spread your skirts, jackets, dresses, and blouses. Transparent plastic cases and bags are indispensable for isolating articles that are apt to be soiled or damp.

As a general rule, it is better to brave a stormy

scene with a husband who believes in travelling light and to take one garment too many rather than one too few. The dress you left behind is bound to be the very one you would have found most useful! Nevertheless, it is especially important when travelling to co-ordinate your wardrobe and to take with you ensembles which have already proven their worth and not a new sweater or dress which does not go with anything you own. Furthermore, it is far more sensible to have several different tops and just one skirt or pair of trousers than the reverse. When travelling by plane, with a minimum baggage allowance and an astronomic charge for overweight, it is vital to be able to combine the different elements of your wardrobe in various ways, thus creating the illusion of many different outfits in a minimum amount of luggage.

LUNCHEONS

The most appropriate outfit for luncheon is a suit of wool, dull silk, or linen, according to the season, since it is always preferable to be too casually rather than too elaborately dressed. For the same reason, it is not advisable to display all your best jewellery, although it is perfectly acceptable to wear pearls or beads, a large clip, and your rings. Your handbag may be quite large, and this is the moment or never to show off your beloved alligator bag! Your shoes may perfectly well have medium rather than high heels, since you will probably want to do some errands during the afternoon without giving the impression of being dressed up in your Sunday best.

After all, the luncheon hour is merely a recess during the working day, and fewer and fewer women lead lives of leisure. And so, even in the most famous, costly, and elegant restaurants, simplicity is the rule at lunchtime.

LUXURY

The word luxury is evocative of all sorts of delight-ful pleasures and comforts, even though its meaning has become somewhat weakened since it has been indiscriminately applied to everything from cocktail sausages to dishwashing powders.

It may be interpreted to mean superfluous, expen-sive, refined, extravagant – in any case, it is a word that caresses the ear as well as the imagination. Its sense is therefore completely subjective. Everyone has his own idea of luxury, just as everyone has his own idea of happiness, from the hobo luxuriating in the warmth of the subway to the art collector revelling in the acquisition of a coveted painting by Picasso. Perhaps the idea of luxury stems basically from a comparison between the minimum standard of living of one group and another. For many women, the sensation of luxury comes simply from the possession of an object that her friends do not own.

We become accustomed to luxury – or at least to our own idea of luxury – much more quickly than to its absence. The flourishing industries which depend upon our desire for luxury cultivate it carefully by advertising designed to convince a larger and larger group of consumers that they can afford 'luxuries.' Dior found it very profitable to place within the buying range of every woman his famous label by selling lipstick under the slogan: 'Your lips at least can be dressed by Dior!'

Where elegance is concerned, the greater the luxury, the more discreet it is – until finally, after advancing through more and more exclusive and restricted stages, you reach the point of ultimate luxury which is imperceptible to everyone but you.

M

MAKE-UP

Make-up is a kind of clothing for the face, and in the city a woman would no more think of showing herself without make-up than she would care to walk down the street completely undressed. Cosmetics are therefore governed by fashion just as clothing is, and the makers of beauty products, like the couture designers, bring out two collections a year of new powders, lipsticks, eye shadows, and nail polish.

Very young women prefer pale lips as well as pale complexions but at the same time extremely accentuated eyes. While a lipstick was practically the equivalent of a young boy's first razor a few years ago, today's teenagers hardly even bother to buy one. And yet every one of them owns a black eyebrow pencil and a set of eye make-up.

Nevertheless, it is still considered bad taste to wear

bright blue or bright green eye shadow during the daytime, and even more so to appear before sunset with scintillating eye cosmetics sparkling with gold or silver.

The fashion in eyebrows is to keep them as natural as possible, groomed but unaltered, and darkened with a pencil only if they are very pale.

For the majority of women who cannot live without lipstick, it is indispensable to own several different colours in order to select the shade which harmonizes best with each different outfit colour. The light pinks with a faint mauve cast go well with all the blue and violet tones; the orange-reds, which are the most fashionable at the moment, are prettier with beiges and yellows; and if you wear a red ensemble, your lipstick should be of exactly the same shade of red.

Very dark lipstick colours are out of style, and so are all the artificial shades too far removed from our natural colouring, such as violet. Neither is it chic to cheat with the natural outline of your lips by painting in a completely new one with a lipstick brush. This useful instrument, by the way, should never be employed anywhere except at your own dressing table.

Ultra-long scarlet fingernails have been, thank heavens, abandoned by elegant women in favour of short, oval nails covered with a colourless polish. However, unless your hands are perfectly lovely, it is probably to your advantage to give them the illusion of greater length by letting your nails grow a little longer and by wearing a light red polish.

In the summertime and out of doors, a skin that is lightly sun-tanned can very well do without make-up, except for a clear bright lipstick. The eyes should only be made up in the evening, because false eyelashes, mascara, and blue eyelids do not get along at all well with brilliant sunshine and even less with sea water.

MATCHMAKING

Because co-ordination is essential to elegance, the fashion stylists attempt to facilitate matters by providing us with various sets of matching accessories and even complete co-ordinated wardrobes. Their efforts are certainly praiseworthy and have contributed a great deal to improving the aspect of our city street scene. But, as in every other phase of elegance, moderation is always the best policy.

If you adore Burberry checks, for instance, you must not let yourself be carried away by the delight of discovering that you can buy a beret, gloves, scarf, sweater, shoes, handbag, and even eyeglass frames in the same check as your new suit! Try to satisfy yourself with a single matched accessory, and your sacrifice will be rewarded by increased elegance.

Solid colours can stand repetition much better than can patterned materials. But even so, an all-navy or all-beige ensemble is less monotonous and more chic if it is relieved by a touch of another colour, or by another shade of the same colour, which is always a foolproof formula.

Having advised you to exercise restraint in fashion matchmaking, I should add that there are a number of cases where matchmaking is without a doubt the elegant thing to do. It is always good fashion to match:

- your raincoat, rain hat, and umbrella.
- your dressing gown and bedroom slippers.
- your luggage, or at least the major pieces.
- your suit blouse and jacket lining.
- a very dressy coat and dress.

Your own good taste and objective eye are the best judges in this matter, because there are no definite rules governing the extent to which you can elegantly match the various elements of a fashion ensemble. Besides, it is not really a very serious error to over-match. Pre-coordinated ensembles and accessories provide a simplified solution to many fashion problems, and their effect is usually quite attractive. But they also betray a certain lack of effort and imagination.

MEN

Appearance is just as important in a man as in a woman. Impressive diplomas and heavy responsibilities are no excuse for not having a good tailor, and only millionaires and geniuses can get away with being badly dressed.

Masculine elegance being synonymous with conservatism, a well-dressed man should NEVER WEAR:

– flashily striped suits.
– shirts in aggressive shades.
– jewellery, including metal bracelets – not even a gold

band on a wrist watch (which is correctly worn only in the daytime).

— trousers that are too tight when slender ones are stylish, or too wide when the fashion pendulum swings to the opposite extreme. The same principle is valid for hats, coat lapels, overcoat lengths, etc.

— a polka dot tie with a striped or plaid jacket.

— a handkerchief that literally floats from the pocket, or one that exactly matches the tie.

— suede shoes in the city, or a cloth cap, both of these accessories being reserved for country wear along with their companions, the tweed jacket and corduroy trousers.

— on the beach: printed shirts and ultra-short shorts (if he is no longer under twenty years of age), socks and closed shoes. The seashore is the only place where a gentleman may wear sandals or espadrilles.

A man should be just as well-groomed as a woman, with his fingernails short and shiny but unlacquered; his beard shaven as many times a day as necessary; and he should smell good only at very close quarters. His hair should not be too long at the nape of the neck, nor hang over the back of his collar; his shirt should be immaculate, his trousers well creased, his jacket unrumpled, and his shoes shined. He should never talk too loudly in public, even if he is highly successful; and he should be adept at making the imperceptible international gesture that calls for a restaurant bill, which he should pay discreetly. He should never tap on his cigarette and he should throw it away when he stops to talk to somebody on the street.

The best-dressed men in the world are the British and the Italians, and in every country today there are bespoke tailors and ready-to-wear inspired by these two styles. But beware! A woman may sometimes be forgiven for being too stylishly dressed, but a man who looks like a fashionplate is unbearable. Elegant, yes. Foppish, no!

(See Sex)

MODELS

To be a fashion model is the dream of many young girls who only see the glamorous side of this career which is, to tell the truth, not as brilliant as it appears to be. In exchange for a few interesting trips each year and the satisfaction of seeing her photograph on the front pages of the newspapers, a model must remain on her feet during hours and hours of fittings, which are called 'posing sessions' and are absolutely exhausting. She doesn't even have the right to gain an extra pound or to acquire a suntan. Except for the extremely photogenic girls who earn a very ample livelihood by posing for fashion magazines in addition to their regular salon duties, the permanent mannequins of a haute couture salon, and even the free-lance fashion models who work on an hourly basis, probably earn less money than a secretary – and they are obliged to invest a much larger portion of their income in their personal appearance.

While actresses can always change their type of role as they grow older, a fashion model is given only one part to play and it lasts only as long as does her youth.

The type of elegance personified by the fashion models is often rather extreme, and it may not seem very easily adaptable to normal life. For example, if a group of models walked down the street attired in their fashion-show ensembles and did not cause every head to turn, the designer would consider his clothes to be a failure. There is an understandable tendency when presenting a collection of fashions to exaggerate a desired effect, to emphasize a certain style. Often this is merely a matter of a few details which can easily be eliminated in order for the ensemble to lose its eccentric air and to become perfectly elegant for an average woman: the hairdo or make-up of the model, who has a naturally striking physical appearance to start with, or simply the oversized or overly brilliant outfit jewellery.

On the other hand, when an ensemble in a fashion show, in a window display, or in a fashion magazine, seems absolutely perfect and if you have fallen in love with it, it is preferable to buy it in its entirety if you do not want to risk being disappointed. A garment presented in a fashion collection is like a picture in a frame. If you remove the frame, the picture is still very beautiful, but all the same, it has lost something.

N

NECKLACES

The ideal necklace, the most universally becoming piece of jewellery ever created, and an indispensable accessory in every woman's wardrobe, is a string of pearls. Every woman should own a single strand pearl necklace and a second one of three or five strands. If she is a *grande dame* of a certain age, she can even wear seven or nine strands. Like roses in a vase, an odd number is more elegant than an even one.

Your pearls may be cultured, imitation, or – in the case of a very few fortunate women – real. But you need not be overly envious of the latter, because they are usually either in a state of terror at the thought of displaying such a costly investment around their necks, or in a state of anguish if they have stored them in a safe, because real pearls must be worn frequently in order to benefit from contact with the skin or else they gradually lose their lustre.

The size and shade of a flattering pearl is a question of one's individual features and complexion tone. In general, the most becoming style for a long slim neck is a rather large, uniform choker; and for a wide neck, a longer, graduated necklace of several strands. In any case, the string should always be knotted in between each pearl for reasons of security, but the knots should be quite small, so that the pearls will lie close together in order to give forth their full lustre.

The choice of a clasp is very important, since a beautiful jewelled clasp on a necklace of more than two strands can also be worn at the front of the neck or near the shoulder, and you will have the impression of owning two or three different necklaces.

A gold necklace is really elegant only when the workmanship is superb, especially if it is of an antique design or studded with semi-precious stones. The plain machine-made gold link chain, whose value lies more in its carat weight than in the artistry of the goldsmith, is never very chic.

The priceless jewelled heirloom necklaces which used to be handed down from one generation to the next in aristocratic families are very rarely seen today, except at a few elegant private balls and on certain state occasions. Even then, many a Parisian society beauty rushes to the place Vendôme the morning after such an event in order to return a set of emeralds or rubies to the jeweller who loaned it to her for just one evening.

At the same time, the vogue for outfit jewellery necklaces has reached new heights, even though they are less favoured at the moment than pins and clips. Many scooped-out necklines, strapless necklines, and high, round ones, really need to be completed by a necklace. The only kind to be avoided are rhinestones, which are almost always an attempted imitation of a diamond necklace and are therefore, like all kinds of imitations, the height of inelegance. However, when the rhinestones are combined with coloured stones or pearls, especially in a reproduction of an antique style, they can add a great deal of originality and brilliance to an evening ensemble.

Pearls or a gold necklace (less chic) can be worn from early in the morning, and a simple necklace of outfit jewellery or semi-precious stones such as turquoise and coral from lunchtime on.

If you lack confidence in your own taste, you

should know that it is always safe and perfectly chic to wear:

- with a suit and sweater: in the city, pearls, in the country, pearls or larger coloured beads.
- with a coloured dress: pearls, or several strands of coloured beads in an attractive harmony, for example, yellow beads with an orange dress, coral with pale blue, turquoise with beige, and jade with navy blue.
- with a black dress: three strands of pearls.
- with a print dress: pearls, or coloured beads which underline one of the shades in the print.

Jet necklaces are smart only when they are worn with white ensembles. White beads are elegant only in the summer – with the exception (need I add?) of pearls.

(See Jewellery)

NECKLINES

The most noticeable part of a dress by far is its neckline. As a matter of fact, when a woman is seated behind a restaurant table, it is the only part of her dress that shows.

From the turtle-neck collar to the strapless top, all sorts of different necklines have enjoyed their hour of glory at one time or another throughout the history of fashion, including even a daring style that completely bared the bosom. The only certainty about the fashion future of necklines is that what is out of date today will probably be the rage tomorrow.

- V necklines are really elegant only if they are exaggeratedly low-cut, almost to the waist.
- the trapeze neckline, which has been neglected during the past few years, is nevertheless one of the most flattering of all; the same is true of strapless evening tops.

Generally speaking, extremely low-cut necklines are more attractive when they are worn by tall, slightly plump women than by small, skinny ones.

V necklines are made to order for very generous busts, on condition that the V is not so deep that it exposes the 'cleavage' in the middle; furthermore, if you are quite short, the waistline should be as high as possible in order to lengthen the over-all silhouette.

Even when they were in fashion, strapless gowns were more becoming to tall women than to short ones. You only need to make the experiment of adding two shoulder straps to one of these strapless bodices in order to observe that you seem to have magically grown at least four inches taller.

Asymmetrical necklines are rather difficult to wear, and are really at their best only on evening dresses draped in the Grecian style.

The bateau neckline is one of the most feminine of all and is becoming to almost every woman. It is the ideal background for showing off a pair of beautiful shoulders and a lovely back with nice, flat shoulder blades. If, however, your shoulder blades are prominent, it is better to have the back cut in a V, so that only the middle of the spine is bared.

Cowl necklines, softly draped either in front or in back, are also an excellent camouflage for a rounded back or for a heavy bust.

Low-cut dresses should never be seen in the city in the daytime. Even when the temperature soars, a revealing décolletage, as alluring and refined as it may be for evening wear, seems to be a sign of poor taste in bright daylight and even somewhat indecent.

NEGLIGEES

One of the most baffling points of inconsistency in many otherwise elegant women is the way they completely neglect their appearance during the hours of intimacy in their own homes – which is the very time and place they ought to be the most attractive.

Almost every woman owns one or two really lovely nightgown and negligee ensembles, which she carefully saves for travelling. The hotel room-service waiters don't know how lucky they are! And when you think that a really well trained room waiter isn't even supposed to glance at the lovely lady in her pretty lingerie – what a waste!

O

OCCASIONS

There are numerous occasions in life when even the most unassuming, least clothes-conscious woman realizes that it can be of real importance socially for her to be well dressed. Suddenly seized with panic at the idea that she will be the centre of attention, she wonders in anguish, 'Whatever shall I wear?' and rushes out to buy any kind of new dress at all.

Whatever the ceremony at which you or your husband may be required to play a leading role – such as godparent at a christening, chairman of a banquet in honour of a distinguished guest, committee member of a charity ball, at your child's graduation, at a birthday dinner, the awarding of an honour to your husband, or merely as a guest at the Christmas office party – you should always adopt simplicity as the best policy and not try to radically transform your appearance for this special event.

For example, if you live in tailored suits, flat heels, and horn-rimmed spectacles during three hundred and sixty-four days of the year, don't suddenly wear a fancy bow in your hair and a low-cut red dress trimmed with ruffles and lace. If, on the other hand, everyone is used to seeing you sparkling from morning till night with jewellery and vivid colours, don't arrive all draped in black as if you were on your way to a funeral. It would only astonish everyone, and on this particular occasion you do not want to cause a sensation, but simply to present a pleasing and attractive appearance.

The first consideration to guide you in your choice of clothes should be the hour of the ceremony, and afterward its degree of formality, and the setting in which it is to take place.

Black is not the ideal colour for more or less ceremonious late-day and formal evening functions; it is, in fact, prohibited by Court protocol. But nothing better has ever been invented for the smart little dinner dress, without sleeves and somewhat décolleté, that is perfect to wear when the men are in dark business suits rather than black tie. A chic black dress of this type is an indispensable part of every woman's wardrobe, and it is ideal for all those business dinners when your husband wishes to proudly introduce to his boss, colleagues, or customers, a wife whose good taste is as remarkable as her elegance.

When entertaining in your own home, no matter how wealthy or important your guests may be, it is never nice to attempt to dazzle them. Besides, it is very bad politics to eclipse your women guests by wearing a particularly stunning or expensive gown, for it might only inspire jealousy, and heaven knows the ill that can be wrought by a jealous woman! In trying *too* hard to dress and entertain with elegance, you can sometimes inadvertently inspire the resentment of the very people you are trying to impress . . .

ORIGINALITY

In order to be elegant, a woman must begin by knowing how to make a wise selection from among the multitude of clothes that are offered for sale at every price. If to this science she is able to add the gift of inventing personal details – such as the placement of a jewel, or an unexpected combination of colours – she then becomes a fashion leader and one of those rare women who set a style to be followed by others (as we say in the fashion business, she is a 'loco-motive').

I think that there is probably no more than one woman in 200,000 who is endowed with this innate talent, which inspires her, for example, to unearth an old egg basket in the attic and transform it into a beach bag, or to wear her grandfather's pocket watch around her neck on a long chain – to cite only two examples of fashion which were very quickly popu-larized, but which were certainly invented by some clever woman whose original idea was imitated.

Originality, when it is only the desire to attract attention, has acquired a somewhat unfavourable meaning, especially in a society which is becoming increasingly conformist. And it is true that when originality lacks taste and moderation, it can indeed lead to comic effects justifiably feared by most women who, in order to be sure of not making a mistake, prefer to dress like everybody else in the most banal manner.

However, fashion can only be renewed by a con-tinuous stream of original experiments, which cease to shock as soon as they have been adopted by a certain number of people. As Jean Cocteau has said,

'Fashion is the acceptance of the ridiculous.' What was at first original then becomes 'the fashion'; it is abandoned by its creators as soon as it has been generally adopted, and the greater its success, the more rapid is its decline. Out of twenty original ideas, perhaps only one – and not necessarily the most worthy – will survive. But without the inventive women and designers who refuse to be just like everybody else, fashion would cease to exist.

P

PERFUME

Humanity has always felt the need to flatter its olfactory sense, and as proof you only need to visit the Louvre or the Metropolitan Museum and admire the cases full of antique perfume vials which date from the most ancient civilizations. However, taste in perfume has taken many different forms throughout the world and throughout history.

For example, in the African bush country, even the most primitive tribes concoct perfumes which are potent enough to kill every fly on Fifth Avenue. At the time of Louis XIV, when it was necessary to mask the body odours that resulted from the general lack of hygiene, perfumes were much stronger than they are today. In fact, the modern trend has been more and more toward lighter scents, and toward an increased use of toilet waters and colognes in preference to more concentrated essences. Today it is considered very bad taste if a woman's presence can be perceived by scent before it is observed by sight, even if her arrival is announced by Miss Dior. It is also inelegant to leave in one's wake a trail of heady perfume, like the exotic heroine of a pre-World War I novel. Because of this vogue for lighter scents, many women who remember the perfume their mothers used to wear claim that modern blends are less lasting than they used to be. This may or may not be so, but in any case it cannot be too great an objection because the perfume industry is booming.

Two principal factors influence a woman in her choice of a perfume. First, the container – which she enjoys displaying on her dressing table if the bottle is elegant, obviously expensive, and if it bears a famous label and secondly, the scent itself, if it underlines her personality and adds to her allure. In this regard, the only danger to beware of is a chemical incompatibility between certain perfume essences and certain skins. Consequently, the best way to select a perfume is by a method of trial and error; the best way to apply it is with an atomizer; and the height of refinement is to have your toilet water, perfume, hand soap, bath salts, dusting powder, and even sachets for your lingerie drawer, all scented with the same perfume.

In my mother's day, once you had discovered a perfume that pleased you as well as your entourage, it was advisable to stick to it. An elegant woman usually considered it a point of honour to remain faithful to her perfume, which she considered as a sort of signature. But now it seems that perfumes follow a more varied pattern; some are designed for young women or for not so young ones; some are made for summer, others for cooler weather. So an elegant woman, though she cannot change her scent every other day, because her clothes would become impregnated with a dreadful mixture, is not as faithful as she used to be. On the contrary, she is always delighted to receive a gift of a new perfume.

PERSONALITY

To be elegant is first of all to know oneself, and to know oneself well requires a certain amount of reflection and intelligence. Consequently, a woman who is utterly stupid will always find it extremely difficult to become truly elegant. She will imitate any fashion that happens to strike her fancy, without attempting to adapt it to her particular case, to her particular figure, or to her particular life – even when the fashion in question was obviously created for a type of woman entirely different from herself.

It requires a certain strength of character in order to disengage your own personality from the setting or the entourage that may confine it, often out of an affectionate desire to offer you protection. Some women never do succeed in liberating themselves, or else only very late in life. But nowadays, even very young girls are free from parental supervision, and they tend to be attracted by everything that is the opposite of what they have known at home. This form of conditioning is perhaps just as valid as another, and probably results in exactly the same proportion of elegant and slovenly women as before, because I have often noticed that the daughter of a very fashionable woman usually likes to dress like a tramp; while the daughter of a mother who is always dressed in blue jeans, will dream of nothing but lace and ruffles!

Personality is not only a revolt, but also the recognition of all of one's physical defects and qualities, as well as one's moral and financial resources. Which means that you should recognize the fact that:

- if you haven't the courage to walk past a building under construction where twenty workmen are sure to whistle at you, there is no point in buying the stunning red hat that was so becoming to you.
- if you have very difficult hair which holds a new set for an hour at the most, you might as well decide right now on a hair style that you can arrange yourself, such as a chignon or a French twist, rather than attempt to copy the elaborate coiffure of the woman next door.
- if you are five feet tall and weigh 130 pounds, it is better to put away your flat-heeled shoes until the weekend.
- if your husband simply hates to go out in the evening, and if you do not wish to hurt his feelings, it is useless to buy a beautiful evening coat, even at a marked-down price; on the other hand, a lovely new negligee might help to enliven those dull evenings at home.
- if you are a basketball champion, you will probably look ridiculous in a hand-tucked pastel chiffon blouse.

In short, developing a personality means knowing everything about oneself and, above all, avoiding the ostrich method of refusing to recognize what is most disagreeable in one's life or in one's physical appearance, but instead, trying to remedy it. Once a woman has defined her personality – or, if she has more character, moulded it to her taste – she will find it easier to achieve not only elegance but also happiness.

PHOTOGRAPHY

I do not know a single woman who has ever thought she looked her best in an amateur snapshot. However, it is often her own fault, because in seeking to be a good sport and to behave naturally, she has not been willing to pose like a professional model.

Although it is hardly advisable to assume the exaggerated poses that fashion photographers are obliged to invent in order to produce startling and original magazine layouts, you should nevertheless realize that:

- you should stand straight with your toes turned outward, with one leg placed a little ahead of the other, and with your body turned slightly sideways, so that the camera will capture a three-quarters view.
- unless you are very young, you should always smile at the photographer; otherwise, the expression lines

around the mouth are apt to make you look disagreeable and tired.

- you should always remove your dark glasses for an outdoor snapshot, but never look directly into the sun.
- if you are being photographed stretched out on a beach or the deck of a boat, it is more flattering to prop yourself up on one hip and an elbow and present your body in profile, instead of lying spread out flat like a fried egg.
- the most frequently recommended position for the hands – lightly crossed on your lap – always seems terribly stiff; if you don't know what to do with them, you can place them behind your back, but never on your hips.
- it is better for the camera to be angled at you from a low position rather than from above, which always has a foreshortening effect.
- group photographs, in which a row of wooden Indians gaze with frozen smiles at the little birdie in the camera, are always slightly comical.
- if you are a prominent celebrity being photographed for the newspapers, do not hesitate to insist on showing only your best profile. You can be sure that the film star who has been 'surprised' by the photographers during a shopping spree has carefully

posed at least five or six times for each different shot, and that is why the final result seems so natural! It is far better to appear slightly ridiculous in front of a handful of people during five or ten minutes, than to hundreds of thousands of newspaper readers the following morning.

A family album is a charming tradition, but it can also sometimes be highly embarrassing. Take my advice and re-edit it every ten years or so.

Finally, when you have a portrait photograph made, you should wear your most classic and conservative dress and jewellery, and even then attempt to conceal your clothing as much as possible, because it can date a picture more quickly than anything else; and be sure to arrange your hair in a simple style for the same reason.

PLANNING

The best-dressed women are often those who devote the most thought (which does not necessarily imply the most time, and certainly not the most money) to their clothes.

Twice a year, as the summer draws to a close in

September, and as the first welcome signs of spring appear at the end of February or early in March, it is a good idea to make an inventory of your wardrobe for the coming season. You must be perfectly objective and ruthlessly discard:

- worn or stained materials, and outdated garments that are not worth remodelling.
- worn-out shoes and handbags that you have been saving for a rainy day.
- hats that have gone out of style.

And you should plan to give away:

- clothes that have become too small. (by the time you have lost weight, they will probably be outmoded anyway).
- anything that you haven't worn for the past two years and cannot remodel into a useful garment; and in this regard, you should not expect miracles from dyeing or major transformations, because the results are frequently disappointing and always expensive.

For the rest, make arrangements for the necessary repairs: adjusting the length of a hemline to the current mode, replacing buttons, etc. And then decide what you will need to buy in order to complete your wardrobe.

It is often practical to select a basic colour for each season. It might be beige, navy blue, grey, or black-and-white checks for the spring; black, brown, dark grey or dark green for the winter. It is not a bad idea to have several ensembles in the same colours so that they can be worn with the same accessories.

At the beginning of the season, you should already have acquired your basic ensembles for the major occasions in your life: career or daytime clothes, evening, and sportswear. Try to think ahead also of any special trips you may be planning, as well as special events like weddings or balls that may be on your social calendar. If you have chosen your major items such as a winter coat and a spring suit with care and not in a desperate last-minute frenzy, you can succumb later on to a spur-of-the-moment purchase with no risk of unbalancing your entire wardrobe or of spending your entire budget on an extra tailored suit when it is a dinner dress you really need! You should also try not to make the same major purchases each year, but buy a good coat one year, for example, and the next a tailored suit or a dressy outfit.

It would be a mistake, however, to establish a wardrobe programme and adhere to it inflexibly. Some of the most becoming ensembles have been bought on an impulse. A woman should never deprive herself of something that will give her pleasure and make her more beautiful simply because it was not a part of her well-laid plans.

POSTURE

Years ago, every well-bred young girl was given posture lessons, and even today when we send our young daughters to dancing school it is usually in the hope that they will grow up to be graceful young women rather than prima ballerinas.

The models who present a fashion collection adopt a curious kind of extremely unnatural walk and posture, with their shoulders slightly hunched, their tummies hollowed, and their hips shoved forward, to form a kind of figure S. They glide rather than walk, and the entire effect is deliberately striking and artificial. But you can be sure that as soon as these beauties leave the salon spotlight, they assume a perfectly natural walk and posture.

In normal life, it is always to a woman's advantage

to hold herself straight, as if she wished to stretch her height by several inches, even if she is already very tall. A rounded back, sagging shoulders and a drooping chin create an image of extreme lassitude, or discouragement with life . . . and of being ten years older than you really are.

When a woman is trying on clothes, she almost always holds herself beautifully erect in front of the dressing room mirrors. If afterward she hollows her chest and lets her entire body slump, she should not be surprised to find that her new dress does not look at all as chic as it did when she tried it on in the shop.

POUNDS

The unwanted pound which insidiously sneaks up on you when your attention is elsewhere is the most redoubtable enemy of many women. Every springtime the fashion magazines and women's pages invent new diets which, if they are followed to the letter, guarantee a slender figure and, consequently, elegance. Although it isn't necessarily indispensable to be as skinny as a fashion model in order to be elegant, it is probably true that the list of the Ten Best Dressed Women is also a list of the Ten Hungriest Women.

According to the particular diet theory you happen to believe in, the Enemy may take the form of salt, liquids, sugar, fats, starches, fruit, vegetables, cheese, certain meats, sweets, or alcohol – alas, the list of appetizing dishes that can be enjoyed without risk of obesity is shrinking sadly every year! If children's fairy tales are one day brought up to date, the good fairy should not be allowed to forget, when she waves her wand over the crib of the little princess, to endow her with the magical power of being able to eat anything she wishes without putting on weight.

Slimming is practically a new religion, whose rite is the twenty-four-hour fast, whose high priests are the medical specialists, and whose pope is Dr Atkins. It used to be practised very discreetly, almost clandestinely, and the early followers contented themselves with a moderate slenderness which still allowed for a few soft curves. But the sect has gained new converts every day until it now confidently decrees that salvation is impossible for the few remaining infidels who do not believe in the stringbean silhouette and the skinny look. Is it all because of our small modern apartments or because of the population explosion? (The thinner people are, the less room they will take up.) It is difficult to say. However, it is ironic that the thinner we are supposed to be, the more fattening modern life becomes, for nervous overweight is certainly one of the maladies of the century. (And because overweight is so often a form of malady, you should consult only your doctor for advice on reducing diets.)

And so most women follow diets practically all their lives, and the quantity of our meals has been cut in half during the past thirty years. However, it can sometimes be a good idea to forget to count your calories. For example, a woman who nibbles on an apple in a smart restaurant vexes the man who invited her as well as the maître d'hôtel – and who knows if the former won't prefer to share his table the next time with a lady who is perhaps less sylphlike, but also less ascetic.

Moral: Dieting should be practised in solitude.

PROSPERITY

A charming customer said to me one day as she was admiring two rings I wear, one of them since my engagement and the other since I lost my mother, and undoubtedly imagining that a woman is reduced to working in a couture salon only after serious financial reverses, 'My dear, how wise you were to at least hang onto your jewels!'

At the time, her remark struck me as being very funny; but all the same, it was quite pertinent, for there are too many women who do not know how to take advantage of a moment of financial splendour by acquiring their essential possessions. A few pieces of good jewellery, top-quality handbags, a gold compact, or a lovely umbrella, may in the long run render more service than six dresses in the latest fashion from an expensive designer. It's worth remembering. The stock market isn't always rising, and it may sometimes be necessary to coast along for several years on what you already own without appearing to be any less elegant.

PUBLIC APPEARANCE

The glare of footlights and photographers' flash bulbs is no longer reserved for actresses and political candidates. Even the most retiring type of woman may one day find that her civic or philanthropic activities unexpectedly lead her onto the centre of the stage.

Your choice of clothes depends primarily on the time and place of the event in question. In general, you should prefer an ensemble which is very well designed, simple in line and clean in silhouette, of a dull rather than shiny material, one that has a certain amount of body. Clinging crêpes are therefore not particularly advisable; and floating materials such as chiffon look lovely in motion, but lose a great deal of their charm when you are obliged to remain standing still. Black is not an ideal choice, and it is better to avoid prints entirely. For daytime events, I would recommend one of the neutral shades, worn with a subtle harmony of accessories; and for the evening, the bright, clear colour which is most becoming to you. A neckline that is cut away from the base of the neck, which it tends to elongate, creates a flattering frame for the face.

If you wear evening clothes, your hair should be clean and shining, arranged as simply and smoothly as possible.

If you must remain standing for a long time, it is advisable to consider comfort as well as elegance when you select the shoes that you will wear. And if you are to speak in front of a microphone, you should leave your dangling charm bracelet at home, for it is certain to provide unwanted sound effects. Brilliant outfit jewellery may be effective behind the footlights, but it does not photograph very well; if photographers are present, it is better to wear rather discreet jewellery and especially pearls, which are both elegant and photogenic.

Eyeglasses are another accessory which reflect the spotlights and can spoil a picture; try to leave your glasses in your handbag, unless you literally cannot see a thing without them.

It is a good idea to stage a private dress rehearsal in front of a full-length mirror in order to make sure that you haven't overlooked a single detail. You can then forget about your clothes and devote your entire attention to your audience – which is, after all, one of the principles of elegance in private as well as in public.

(See Occasions)

Q

QUALITY

A quality shop which wishes to be considered as such refuses to tolerate bad taste within its walls.

Of course, in an inexpensive store that cannot run the risk of losing sales, extremely chic articles keep company with depressingly ordinary ones. But a luxury establishment should offer nothing but quality merchandise. Only then can a customer have confidence in the label and thus purchase at the same time her wardrobe and her peace of mind.

In the haute couture it is unkind, to say the least, to sell a customer a garment in which she looks ridiculous. It is better, no matter what the cost, to refuse stubbornly to sell it to her, even though she may be just as persistent in wanting to buy it. This, at least, has always been my personal credo. But I am not sure that all salespeople have the perseverance to hold their ground in the face of a customer's opposition. Many of them are so concentrated on making a sale that they never stop to consider the disastrous publicity represented by a badly dressed customer. Not only is the client lost forever (because she will never admit that it was she who insisted, in the face of contrary advice, on the unbecoming model); but besides, all of her friends will spread the word everywhere that there is really no point in paying the prices of such and such a designer if it is only to be turned into such a frump!

So for once commercial and aesthetic interests are identical, and a quality shop should never have to blush at what passes through its doors. This is one of the guarantees it offers its clientele – which is why the word 'quality' is often synonymous with 'expensive.' Often, but not always – and even less so in these days of technical progress. Once upon a time, you only had to hint that a material contained rayon in order for the customers to turn up their noses. But by now all women are aware of the miraculous advantages of the man-made fibres, and former standards of quality have been adjusted to them. Besides, now that so many elegant ensembles are made from materials which were formerly reserved for utility wear – such as mattress ticking, blue jeans, and cotton – you might say that design has become more important than material and that the meaning of quality when applied to a dress has shifted from an idea of solidity toward one of elegance and comfort.

Only a handful of women can afford to have everything in their wardrobe of the very finest quality, but every budget can be stretched to cover a few basic luxury items, preferably those where quality represents a long-term investment and often means a saving in the end. An obvious example is a made-to-measure tailored suit, or a classic fine leather handbag – an expensive Hermès model is good for ten years! And there are all the other quality accessories that can add prestige to an entire ensemble, for example:

- a lovely umbrella (if you don't have the habit of losing them).
- a cashmere sweater.

And finally, if you can afford just one garment from the best shop in town, let it be a coat. Not only can it be worn on a maximum number of occasions, but it is the one garment whose impressive label will be seen by everybody!

QUANTITY

One of the most striking differences between a well-dressed American woman and a well-dressed Parisienne is in the size of their respective wardrobes. The American would probably be astonished by the very limited number of garments hanging in the Frenchwoman's closet, but she would also be bound to observe that each one is of excellent quality, expensive perhaps by American standards, and perfectly adapted to the life the Frenchwoman leads. She wears them over and over again, discarding them only when they are worn or outmoded, and she considers it a compliment (as it is meant to be) when her best friend says, 'I'm so glad you decided to wear your red dress – I've always loved it!'.

Americans are often shocked by the high prices in the Paris shops, and they wonder how a young career girl, for example, who earns half of the salary of her American counterpart, can afford to carry an alligator handbag and to wear a suit from the Balmain boutique. The answer is that she buys very few garments; her goal is to possess a single perfect ensemble for each of the different occasions in her life, rather than a wide choice of clothes to suit every passing mood.

An elegant Frenchwoman expects her coats to last for three years at least, her suits and dresses at least two years, and her evening clothes almost indefinitely. She owns very few sets of lingerie at one time, but she replaces them frequently. The same is true of her shoes and gloves, while her handbags last for years and years. It is only her vacation wardrobe that she renews every summer, most often buying these expendable items ready-made in a department store or an inexpensive boutique.

Of course, these two different attitudes spring from two different ways of life, and it is undeniable that the American woman is constantly surrounded by new temptations and assailed by the most irresistible kind of fashion advertising. Moreover, she has been told that her role in the national economy is to continually buy and consume.

And yet, I wonder if she wouldn't profit by replacing once in a while her penchant for quantity with a quest for quality. She might find that not only is her elegance increased, but also the enjoyment and even the confidence that she gets from her clothes.

QUOTATIONS

ON DRESS:

'Costly thy habit as thy purse can buy, but not expressed in fancy; rich, but not gaudy, for the apparel oft proclaims the man.' (*Shakespeare*)

ON ELEGANCE:

'Elegance is something more than ease – more than a freedom from awkwardness and restraint. It implies a precision, a polish, and a sparkling which is spirited, yet delicate.' (*Hazlitt*)

ON FASHION:

'Every generation laughs at the old fashions, but follows religiously the new.' (*Thoreau*)

'There may often be less vanity in following the new modes than in adhering to the old ones.' (*Joubert*)

'Fashion is only the attempt to realize art in living forms and social intercourse.' (*Oliver Wendell Holmes*)

'Excess either way shocks, and every wise man should attend to this in his dress as well as language; never be affected in anything, but follow, without being in too great haste, the changes of fashion.' (*Molière*)

'Be not too early in the fashion, nor too long out of it; nor at any time in the extremes of it.' (*Lavater*)

ON TASTE:
'Bad taste is a species of bad morals.' (*Bovee*)

'Taste is, so to speak, the microscope of judgment.' (*Rousseau*)

'A truly elegant taste is generally accompanied by excellence of heart.' (*Fielding*)

R

RAIN

To be elegant during stormy weather simply carry an umbrella. This useful accessory can be a very lovely object, evidence of your refinement; or it can be the glaring proof of hopelessly bad taste. It is wiser to resist such fancies as:

- umbrella handles of imitation mother-of-pearl, or elaborately adorned silver and gilt.
- sugary pastel colours such as mauve, rose, pea green, and baby blue.
- prints.
- folding umbrellas that dangle from the wrist.

Crook handles are more practical than straight ones because they can be hooked over the arm, while straight handles, which are often prettier, either immobilize one hand or slide to the ground if you try to hold them under your arm. Beige is one of the best colours for umbrellas, as it is for raincoats, because it harmonizes with almost any outfit and casts a particularly flattering shadow on the face. Black and white are safe, classic choices. As a general rule it is best to avoid raincoats made of waterproof satin or similar which skillful salesgirls try to persuade you to buy on the grounds that they can be worn as an evening coat as well as a raincoat. The truth is that they are seldom really elegant in either role.

When leaving on a trip, it is a good idea to carry your raincoat and umbrella with you in your hand baggage, instead of packing them in your suitcase. For some mysterious reason, it almost always seems to be at the moment of arrival that you need them most!

Finally, you should choose from your wardrobe on a rainy day only materials that are not likely to be damaged by the rain, instead of attempting to protect your handbag, hat, and shoes by means of transparent plastic covers. These useful but unaesthetic inventions should be left where they belong – on the display shelves of the supermarket, or, in the form of garment bags and cases, in your storage closet and bureau drawers.

RESTAURANTS

In most cities, there are two different categories of restaurants: the ones where you go in order to be seen, and those where you go in order to enjoy a marvellous meal. There is no need to speak of the restaurants where you go merely to be fed, usually at lunchtime, and where simplicity is obligatory. But in all the other cases, a woman who wishes to be considered elegant should change her clothes before going out to dine in a restaurant.

Of course, you wouldn't dress the same for dinner at an elegant spot as you would for a meal in a modest neighborhood bistro. In the first type of restaurant, where you expect to be seen, you can wear your most sumptuous ensembles, eat caviar, and drink champagne, without the slightest risk of appearing vulgar, because the setting has been designed for just such luxury. But in the other type, where you go only for the amusement of trying some extraordinary new dish or merely an exceptionally well-prepared plate of spaghetti and meatballs, it is preferable to be less elaborately attired and to drink ordinary red wine!

Between these two extremes, there is a wide variety of restaurants ranging from the fashionable bistro of the moment, where a sophisticated outfit such as a chic black crêpe sheath in the very newest fashion from a smart boutique is the thing to wear, and where the food is usually mediocre, to the famous, long-established restaurant noted for its food, where the customers are hearty eaters, plump, provincial, well-to-do, relaxed . . . and not terribly elegant. In the latter kind of place, you can wear whatever you own that is most banal and plush. They are excellent passports for this particular kind of establishment.

In other words, it is indispensable to know where you are going to be taken to dinner before you dress to go out in the evening.

RICH

At the very time when the economic prosperity of many countries has never been so spectacular, it happens to be considered bad taste to give the impression of being rich. Even the words 'rich' and 'opulent' have acquired a rather pejorative sense, whether they are applied to the decoration of a living room or to a woman's figure. A close relation to 'ostentatious,' they have become synonymous with 'vulgar' and 'inelegant'.

True opulence, like true luxury, should be practically imperceptible – except to the eyes of the initiated few who can recognize at a glance that a simple little navy blue reefer is a Balenciaga original which probably cost as much as a fur coat.

RINGS

A diamond ring is the only form of diamond jewellery that can be correctly worn before lunch-time. Since it often happens that the only rings a woman possesses are her diamond engagement ring and a wedding band, it is well worthwhile selecting them with the greatest care. Sometimes it is advisable to modify the original design or even to replace the stones or setting entirely, as one's taste and finances improve throughout the years and as fashions change.

Diamonds may be set in either gold or platinum with equal elegance, and the wedding band should of course match the setting of the engagement ring. A diamond may be cut in various ways: generally speaking, the marquise (boat-shaped), emerald-cut (square or oblong, with squared-off corners), and pear (teardrop-shaped) forms are more flattering to short fingers, which they appear to lengthen and slenderize. The beauty of brilliant-cut (many-faceted, requiring a high setting), and square-cut stones is best enhanced by long, slender hands. But it is also true that the design and setting can often create miraculous optical illusions in adapting a certain stone to a certain type of hand. Moreover, a rather small solitaire is always more elegant when it forms part of a composition with other gems or brilliants, than when it stands rather forlornly all alone.

The mode in rings has followed the trend of all jewellery, and it is fashionable to combine two or more different kinds of precious stones, such as sapphires, emeralds, and diamonds; a black pearl and a white one with diamonds; rubies, sapphires, and diamonds; or – the ultimate in elegance and luxury – canary yellow and white diamonds.

A solitaire ring of a stone other than diamonds is somewhat risky. The truth is that an enormous topaz or aquamarine is never supremely elegant, even though I have seen them worn by some very fashionable women – and even though the topaz is one of the loveliest gems of all. On the other hand, a large star sapphire is a jewel of great beauty and elegance.

It is unwise to wear more than a single ring on each hand (with your wedding and engagement rings counting as one). And it is only sensible to realize that a ring becomes soiled more quickly than any other piece of jewellery and that no amount of scrubbing with a toothbrush can replace a professional jeweller's cleaning and polishing once a year.

(See Jewellery)

ROYALTY

Always on exhibition, but with less freedom than the movie stars, royal personages are obliged to adhere to rather impersonal rules of elegance.

The British Royal Family is certainly the most prominent and the most discussed. Queen Elizabeth, without going so far in the direction of starchy stiffness as her grandmother Queen Mary, is nevertheless always very conservative and regal in her manner of dress, and to imitate her would be disastrous for any other woman. Her over-trimmed hats, her open-toed shoes (too often white), and her fur cape-stoles are the weak points in her wardrobe. It must be admitted too that she is badly corseted, and that the wide ribbon decorations she is obliged to wear do nothing to improve her evening dresses, which are often already too ornately embroidered. On the other hand, her jewels are marvellous, her hair style is natural and becoming, and she possesses that radiantly flawless English complexion. The time she was most elegant was certainly the day she visited the Pope, dressed all in black as dictated by protocol – the same protocol which prevents her from wearing black on any other occasion, except for funerals. All in all, these are only minor criticisms, because it must be exceedingly difficult, if not impossible, to be the Queen of England and at the same time an elegant woman.

In any case, the Queen is far more elegant than her sister, Princess Margaret, was who, by trying too hard to be chic, succeeded in being neither regal nor elegant but only conspicuous.

The Duchess of Kent is always perfect in her appearance, as she has been for years. Englishwomen have become much more interested in clothes, and above all much less insular in their taste, and when an Englishwoman decides to be pretty, she is the most beautiful woman in the world.

The most popular and the most admired of all such prominent ladies was not quite a queen, but maybe even more, because she added a strong personality to her official functions. She was, of course, Mrs Jacqueline Kennedy, whom *Women's Wear Daily* referred to as 'Her Elegance'. She was never, to my knowledge, caught in a lapse of elegance; she was always youthfully and casually dressed, in a fashion perfectly adapted to modern life, to her official position, and to her individual type.

If every woman dressed as well, there would be no point in writing this book. Furthermore, she exerted a considerable and beneficial influence on American fashions, and while she may not always have bought her wardrobe in Paris, her clothes were nevertheless entirely inspired by the haute couture. The French crowds were so enchanted by her during her official visit to Paris in 1961, that the President at one point introduced himself as 'Jackie's husband'.

S

SALES

Sales days in the Paris couture salons are the occasion for the most incredibly comic spectacle! Plump matrons trying desperately to squeeze into dresses that were made to be worn by the sylphlike mannequins, under the agonized eye of the sales directress, who shivers as she seems to hear the pained cries of splitting seams and the mournful groans of tortured zippers. Customers wandering about in panties and bra without the slightest embarrassment. And, the most frightening of all, the inveterate bargain-seekers, who sail into the salon of Dior or Givenchy as if they were visiting the Flea Market, and who, with knitted brow, determinedly ferret through the garments on display in search of a real pearl.

It is quite possible to find a 'pearl' in the sales if you know how to go about it, if you have no preconceived ideas and are willing to buy a winter coat in June or a linen dress in January, if you consider that it is merely something extra to add to your wardrobe, and last but not least, if you have the figure of a fashion model. Coats are naturally the easiest to fit to almost any size, but they are also the first to be snatched up.

Nevertheless, I would not advise a novice to venture into the couture sales, because if she has the bad luck to fall into the hands of an unscrupulous salesgirl (which happens less often, of course, in a house with a good reputation than in some others), she runs the risk of taking home a garment she will never dare to wear again after the first time she has tried it on in front of her own mirror, far from the intoxicating atmosphere of the salesroom.

The clothes that are placed on sale in the couture salons include not only the models worn by the mannequins during the daily presentation of the season's collection, but also those that have been returned by dissatisfied or fickle customers, perhaps some odds and ends from previous collections, and an occasional unfinished dress or coat that for one reason or another has never been completed. It is only fair to add that the most useful garments are usually reserved at the beginning of the season by regular customers, so that what is left at the end has most often been rejected because of its odd size, difficult colour, or extreme style.

Department-store sales are riskier still, even though fantastic bargains are sometimes possible. First of all, the merchandise is often worn and soiled. If it isn't, the reason is probably that the buyer has purchased an odd lot of discontinued garments especially for the sale. Some manufacturers specialize in sales merchandise, and their wares are seldom worth more than the so-called 'half price' that is asked for them on clearance day.

But I do not expect these sobering facts to dissuade any woman from trying her luck, for bargain-hunting seems to be an innate feminine instinct. You may even get a good deal of satisfaction out of the sales, provided that you are armed with lots of courage and the will power to resist the temptation of some darling little outfit which in the end is terribly expensive when you realize that, while it may have cost you 'nothing', it is worth practically nothing to you.

SEX

We live in a world where science fiction has become reality. Machines can do almost everything we can do, we are nourished more and more synthetically, and slowly but surely we are all becoming robotized. But there is one realm that has remained invulnerable to the attacks of progressive science – one activity that has been practiced with the same rites throughout the ages, and that is the reciprocal conquest of men and women. Ever since Biblical times, even during the least civilized periods of the Middle Ages, men have sought a woman's love and women have been only too happy to surrender it.

Before 1914, the education of young girls was exclusively designed to teach them how to win and hold a man. First of all, the social graces: dancing and etiquette; and then, once a young man had been captured in the web patiently woven by a doting mother, instruction in cooking and good housekeeping, in order to retain exclusive rights to the young man's affections – and to his income.

The social evolution of the past decades has emancipated women and opened up to them careers in which they now compete with men on equal grounds for equal pay. But even this radical innovation has not diminished the eternal attraction of the sexes. The modern woman may be a breadwinner, but her number one objective is still to win a man.

To this end, almost every object in her life is a potential arm, as advertising suggests to us on every billboard, newspaper, and magazine, on every radio and television station, at all hours of the day and night. Products that are related to beauty, such as shampoo, toothpaste, cosmetics, and perfume, are presented to us as indispensable allies in any conquest, and to refrain from buying them is the equivalent of retiring to a convent.

Unconsciously or not, men and women thus indulge in all sorts of artifices in order to attract each other, and the truth is that women almost always employ far less discretion than men. In fact, it is often in attempting to exploit their natural advantages that they destroy all hopes of elegance.

So-called 'sexy' styles are never truly elegant, but only suitable for the vamps of gangster films or comic strips. Besides, the authorities responsible for these exaggerations are neither the fashion designers, who only like the most slender, flat-chested mannequins, nor the garment industry, which has all the trouble in the world trying to lodge a generous bosom in the bodice of a dress that has just arrived from Paris without the slightest sign of a dart in front! No, the promoters of the aggressive poitrine are the brassière manufacturers, who construct and reinforce their creations as solidly as skyscrapers, with the result that those anatomical features which were intended to be soft, natural cushions, have been transformed into veritable armor plate. The collective adoration for the big bust and the publicity given to the measurements of certain celebrities is a phenomenon perhaps worthy of the attention of a psychiatrist, or the jury at a live-stock exhibition – but it certainly has nothing to do with either fashion or elegance.

On the other hand, don't believe that in order to be elegant you must dress with austerity and only wear clothes with high round necklines and unrevealing full skirts like the saintly ladies of the Salvation Army. Evening gowns with extremely low-cut necklines are almost always flattering. And dresses that mould the figure – when they merely suggest the forms they cover rather than expose them, and when they are very well made – can cause every head to turn in admiration. Nevertheless, if you are not absolutely sure of the perfection of your figure, and especially if it is a bit on the generous side, instead of emphasizing it, veil it. You will have everything to gain and nothing to lose. As for the Wonderbra, they are meant to be worn only in absolutely desperate cases, and even then with discretion.

A kind of mythology seems to have been built up concerning men's preferences in fashion, with the result that many a young woman who deliberately dresses to attract masculine admiration often inspires only astonishment. To separate once and for all the fact from the fiction, this is

WHAT IS REALLY ATTRACTIVE TO MEN:
– full skirts, tiny waists, and a long-legged look.
– clothes that are in fashion, but not avant-garde; men follow the fashion trends more than you may realize, and even the *Wall Street Journal* prints articles about fashion.
– almost any shade of blue; white; very pale and very dark grey; certain men hate to see their wives in black; others adore it.

– perfume – but modern men appreciate lighter
perfumes than their fathers did, subtle sophisticated
blends rather than the simpler scents.
– collars on suits and coats.

WHAT MEN *THINK* THEY LIKE:
(but only in the movies)
- revealingly tight skirts and aggressively pointed
bosoms.
- false eyelashes.
- 'femme fatale' lingerie.
- musky, oriental scents.
- spike heels.
- yards of black fringe and miles of red chiffon flounces.

In short, men enjoy being envied, but they hate
feeling conspicuous. And they particularly dislike
vulgarity in the women they love.

SHOES

While fashion designers prepare only two or three
different collections a year, the shoe industry provides
us with a steady stream of original new models that

are created or imported in the hopes of tempting us to buy at least twice as many pairs as a well-dressed woman really needs. So self-restraint is absolutely indispensable in this field, because shoes should be the complement of an ensemble, never an end in themselves.

The most elegant shoes in the world will never 'make' an outfit – in fact, if they are too noticeable, they cannot be elegant. But at the same time, the wrong shoes can totally destroy the chic of an otherwise lovely appearance. In order to simplify matters, you can immediately eliminate certain styles that have no place in an elegant wardrobe:

– too high heels, which unbalance the posture, distort the silhouette, and are extremely vulgar. Even if you are only five feet tall, you should wear heels no higher than 2 or 2½ inches.

– open-toed shoes, which are perhaps comfortable, but on a crowded city street, somebody is sure to step on your toes, and whenever it rains your feet get soaking wet. The open-toed sling-back pump was a best-seller back in the forties, but since then the fashion pendulum has swung heavily in favor of closed pumps, more or less low-cut, a style that has always been and will probably always remain the ideal accompaniment to a city outfit.

— wedge heels, which Frenchwomen only accepted reluctantly during the war when, because of the shortage of leather, the shoe manufacturers were obliged to invent some kind of footwear that could be built on a cork or wooden sole. Nothing is more certain to give you an awkward gait and a heavy leg than a high wedgie. And it is the extreme of bad taste when the wedge is made of transparent plastic, with goldfish or flowers floating about inside.

— ankle straps, which are both unflattering and rather cheap-looking.

— shoes with exaggeratedly pointed toes, whose tips, quite obviously empty, curl skyward after they have been worn a few times; shoes that are adorned with an enormous cabbage rose or a giant bow – in other words, all the kinds of shoes that attract too much attention.

— need I add that run-down heels and muddy shoes are simply impossible?

It is always a good idea to wear beige shoes, the same shade as your stockings, with a very pale dress, for they considerably elongate the silhouette, while white shoes make your feet seem enormous. Bright shoes (red, green, etc.) are only chic with a dressy evening ensemble, or in the form of ballerina slippers to be worn with country cottons, after-ski skirts, and trousers.

Ballerinas or moccasins are, in fact, the obligatory companions to trousers. Even the slightest suggestion of a high heel worn with trousers or shorts can reduce to vulgarity the most refined appearance. As a change, you can try those imaginative Roman barefoot sandals, studded with stones, which are smart when worn with sun-tanned legs and simple summer dresses or trousers at fashionable summer resorts.

Ballerinas are also charming for very young girls (until, let's say, the age of twelve, when they can start to wear a small high heel), as well as for young women in the summertime with full-skirted dresses. But they should never be seen on a city street, even in the middle of August, for they create an impression of negligence, as do all kinds of open sandals in the city. On the other hand, high-heeled pumps are just as out of place in the country, at the seashore, or in the mountains, where they should be worn only in the evening with dressy ensembles.

Two-toned shoes can be extremely smart if both

of the tones are dark: brown and black, grey and black, dark red and black, etc. Brown and white or black and white spectator pumps, however, have never been really elegant, despite their recurrent popularity. The truth is that brown-and-white or black-and-white shoes are only smart for golfing.

Black patent-leather pumps, on the other hand, can be worn with almost everything except for very casual or sports ensembles; they harmonize with the colour of any outfit, including white, navy blue, and brown. They combine very well with a black alligator handbag, if you do not care for matching alligator shoes (which should, moreover, be worn only with a casual ensemble).

With sports outfits, it is preferable to avoid high, slender heels and to choose medium, stacked, or even perfectly flat ones – provided that, with the latter, you do not wear a hat.

In the evening, you should never wear daytime shoes with a real evening gown, or sports shoes with a dressy ensemble – although it is possible to wear some-what dressy shoes with a simple (but not sporty) dress. Every woman's dream is to own a separate pair of shoes in the same material as each of her evening gowns. Unfortunately, this is not often possible, especially if you lead a very busy and elegant social life and own a wide assortment of evening dresses. In this case, the best solution is a pair of satin or brocade pumps in a pale or bright colour which harmonizes with all your dresses or perhaps which matches your evening wrap; plus a second pair of pumps in black satin or silk.

A final word of advice, and the most important of all: Never overly sacrifice comfort in the interests of chic, because shoes that are too tight or ill-fitting inevitably give you a tired and tortured look, which is hardly the impression an elegant woman wishes to create!

(See Accessories)

SHOPPING

Shopping provides the same joys in the city that hunting does in the country – in both cases the huntress is rewarded by bagging the object or animal of her dreams!

Without a doubt it is in the department stores, especially in London or New York, that a woman can find the widest choice of clothing and accessories in every price range and from every country in the world. You only need to spend a day inside Harvey Nichols, Bergdorf Goodman, Saks Fifth Avenue, or Macy's, in order to acquire a complete wardrobe according to your means.

SHORTS

Salesgirls in the sports departments should be required to verify a customer's birth certificate in order to avoid selling a pair of shorts to anybody over forty years of age – or thirty-eight inches around the hips.

And so, if you are not absolutely confident of the length of your legs and the loveliness of your knees, it is better to do without them. Long shorts are the most difficult kind of all to wear, and the 'Boy Scout Look' has never been considered elegant.

Very short shorts can be alluring, provided that you have lovely thighs which are neither too thin, too heavy, nor flabby; and provided also that the shorts do not bare the lower part of the buttocks, and that they are narrow enough in the legs so as not to be indecent. In any case, you should always wear a snug, opaque panty underneath, preferably of the same colour as the shorts.

After sixteen years of age, you should not wear

shorts of any kind except on the beach, the tennis court, or on board a boat.

SKIRTS

The darling of the minimum budget, and one of the major triumphs of the ready-to-wear industry, a skirt can be worn with a sweater or blouse day in, day out, from one end of the year to the other, almost anywhere at all – except on a city street (unless it is covered by a coat). Every woman should own at least one skirt of black wool, one of tweed, and one of a lineny material.

Straight skirts. Indispensable with a long jacket, they are most becoming to women with slim hips and slender thighs.

Flared (gored) skirts. Flattering to every figure and especially kind to prominent derrières, they require a short jacket.

Pleated skirts. The most graceful in movement are sunburst pleats, but the waistline must be tiny; box pleats are the most thickening over the hips.

Full, gathered skirts. The slimmer the waistline, the more charming the effect. They cannot stand a jacket, but they cry for a wide, tight belt.

Wraparound skirts. So simple to put on, and so easy to pack — but, nevertheless, not really practical. Out of fashion at the moment, except when worn over a matching bathing suit.

Culotte skirts. Elegant only as part of a shooting or bowling ensemble.

Long evening skirts, which have been rather neglected in recent years, are beginning to recapture the vogue they enjoyed during the 1930s, and they are once more on their way to becoming the ideal outfit for an evening at home.

When you have discovered the type of skirt that is most flattering to you, it is a good idea to remain faithful to it, even though this may mean owning the identical model in several different fabrics.

With several skirts, blouses, sweaters, and an assortment of belts it is possible to be very attractively dressed and even to create the impression of possessing a rather vast wardrobe, all for a minimum investment.

STARS

Even if she has no ambition to set a style, the mere fact of being a beautiful and famous woman multiplies a star's problems of elegance by twenty-four:

twenty-four hours a day during which the photographer's lenses are spying on her. These modern divinities haven't the right to disappoint their adoring public by revealing a wrinkle, a pound more or less, or by appearing in an unattractive dress. And so, many of the leading stars place themselves entirely in the hands of one particular designer and thus limit their margin of error.

Whether they seek it or not, stars exert an important influence on fashion, and the real danger in imitating them lies in the fact that the idol of the moment is often far from being elegant. It can even be stated with the utmost certainty that the teen-age set, gregarious by nature and limited in funds, invariably chooses to imitate only the sloppiest styles. Although the young starlets who launch a fad may be a profitable source of ideas for the stylists of large department stores, it is wiser for the average woman to beware of these imitations, because nine times out of ten she will miss her mark of elegance by a mile. Besides, true elegance is never anecdotal.

STOCKINGS

Despite the efforts of the stocking manufacturers to diversify their wares, most women wear the same kind of stockings from morning till night and for every occasion. Attempts are made to launch a new mode in nylons twice a year, but while we may be told that the fashionable shade this season is apricot, cognac, or antelope, and that seams are in or out of style (considered chic at one time, they were entirely abandoned and now have been rediscovered) – the fact is that stockings offer little scope for the imagination. The basic trend is for them to be more and more invisible.

Nevertheless, the patterned weave and bright-coloured stockings which Dior was the first to propose for country wear can add an amusing personal note to a sports ensemble; and knee-high patterned socks are gay and charming for very young girls.

However, it is wise and economical to resist the latest novelties for daily wear and to choose just two stocking shades each season: one for daytime and one for the evening. With city clothes, a neutral beige shade which will harmonize with the colour of every outfit is best; and for evening wear, a somewhat paler, sheerer stocking, whose reinforcements at the heels and toes will not show inside your evening shoes. Sheerness and strength, incidentally, depend upon the gauge and denier. The gauge refers to a closeness of the knit, and the higher the gauge number, the stronger the fabric; the denier is the weight of the yarn, and the higher the denier, the coarser, heavier, and stronger is the stocking.

When shopping for stockings, you can eliminate the risk of an unpleasant surprise by selecting the colour in real daylight, because the artificial neon lighting of most department stores make nylon shades seem paler than they really are.

You should avoid wearing dark or reddish nylons with a black ensemble, for the effect is rather drab and dreary; a neutral beige is the most attractive shade with black. While sun-tanned legs look stunning with a white or pastel summer dress, nylons of the same hue are for some reason unattractive with white; again, you will do better to wear a slightly rosy or beige shade.

Sheer nylons are no longer a luxury, and there is only a slight difference between the cheaper and more expensive varieties. They are even less expensive if you take the precaution of buying six pairs at a time in the same shade, and of the correct foot size and leg length. And so there is no longer any excuse for wearing a stocking with a run in it, mended or not. An extra pair permanently kept in your handbag is good insurance in case of an untimely snag.

Unfortunately, one still sees far too many twisted and baggy nylons wrinkling around the ankles and knees. Seamless nylons are more apt to bag than seamed ones, because the latter are usually fully-fashioned, that is to say, knitted flat and shaped by means of diminishing or increasing the stitches, instead of merely by increasing the tension, as is the case of the seamless kind. Even so, it is usually possible to avoid unsightly wrinkles by stretching the stocking as soon as the foot is in place, and not simply from the top.

A woman may consider her legs to be merely utilitarian appendages, but to men they are one of her most seductive features, and it would be foolish to neglect this special attraction. The legs of an elegant woman are as well groomed and as well dressed as all the rest of her.

STOLES, SCARVES AND PASHMINAS

These terms are practically synonymous and designate a straight length of material or fur, longer than it is wide, the stole being the same length as the garment it accompanies while the scarf or pashmina may be much shorter. All three of these accessories always add a note of elegance to the suit, coat, or dress whose warmth they are designed to increase.

They can be made of the same material and colour as the garment, or they can establish a contrasting note. They may be trimmed with fringe or pompoms (riskier), or they may be perfectly plain.

Short women are mistaken if they think they cannot wear stoles. On the contrary, the vertical effect is excellent for their figures, just as it is for heavy women whose width they literally cut in two.

Stoles are just as chic worn with a very casual outfit as with a formal evening dress, and they are as practical in summer as in winter. A matching stole is almost always an ideal companion to a long or short evening dress and often even makes it possible to dispense with wearing a separate evening wrap.

In short, stoles, scarves and pashminas posses innumerable good qualities and not a single defect. As an added advantage, they encourage all the most feminine gestures and permit certain gracious movements of the shoulders, which can be exploited with devastating effect by a romantic-minded woman.

SUITS

A good suit is the foundation of a woman's wardrobe. It is the ideal outfit to wear all day long and at every season. It is therefore advisable not to skimp on your purchase of a new suit, so that you will be able to wear it for several years.

A classic suit is the garment that is most often ordered in the Paris couture salons by customers who prefer to buy their dresses in less expensive shops but who wish their suits to be impeccable. As a result, there is always a traffic jam in the tailoring workrooms, and women often have to wait as long as six weeks or more for a fitting appointment with their favorite tailor.

Whether it is in tweed, linen, or wool, the only requirements of a good suit are an excellent cut, a material that has some body, and a stiff interlining in the jacket. The most delicate point in tailoring is fitting a set-in sleeve, which should be absolutely smooth around the armhole, without the slightest sign of a pucker or a leg-of-mutton effect. If you notice that the sleeve of a made-to-measure suit wrinkles and twists, you should never hesitate to insist upon its being taken apart and reset correctly. It is always better for a sleeve to be too short but well set than for it to fit badly in the armhole. If the underarm has been cut too deeply, which seriously restricts one's freedom of movement, the problem is much more serious; the only remedy is to change the entire front of the suit and this, I am afraid, will require a great deal of insistence!

The length of the jacket, the design of the skirt and neckline, along with such details as buttons and belts, are all questions of mode and therefore subject to change. However, if you have taken care to select a model that is in the long-range general fashion trend rather than a passing fancy, a well-made suit is often wearable for five years or more – especially the Balenciaga models, which are at the same time in advance of the mode and independent from it.

Whatever the current fashion may be, long jackets are more becoming to figures which are rather prominent behind, while tailored collars and lapels have a slenderizing effect on heavy bosoms. On the other hand, flat-chested women are often more elegant in collarless buttoned cardigan jackets, especially the short ones, which are very youthful.

While a suit is generally a casual garment, there are no limits to the extent to which it can be 'dressed up'. It can even be made of embroidered silk and worn with a long skirt to compose a very formal evening ensemble. However, a wool suit should never be accompanied by very dressy shoes such as satin pumps. A simple straw or felt hat in the summer and velvet or wool in the winter would be very chic. With a hat of the latter type, you can add pale kid glacé gloves, a pale silk blouse, a pretty jeweled clip, plain earrings and a pearl necklace – and that is as far as you can go in attempting to dress up a basic suit. An elegant woman does not dress exclusively in suits. Nevertheless, it is one of her most dependable garments, and, when she has very few items in her wardrobe, it is a marvellous all-purpose outfit.

SWEATERS

So many charming sweaters are made today that it would be quite possible for a woman to be elegantly attired from morning till midnight in a wardrobe entirely composed of different sweaters and skirts. Few women can resist the temptation of a soft new pullover in a luscious shade, and how right they are (unless they are afflicted with a very large bust), because it provides them with an inexpensive way of renewing their wardrobe. Besides, a beautiful sweater is always more elegant than a nondescript dress.

But you should not abuse this useful garment. In particular, you should realize that a sweater can also be the contrary of elegance if you have neglected to respect one of the following rules:

- Only solid-coloured sweaters of cashmere or silk (or of similar synthetic materials) are elegant in the city.
- The open neckline of a V-neck sweater should always be filled in with a scarf unless it is worn over a blouse or pullover.
- Only one kind of embroidery or appliqué is chic in

the daytime: naïve or Tyrolean-type trimmings on winter sports sweaters.

- Heavy knits, stripes, cable stitching, Jacquard patterns, and all kinds of eccentric designs should preferably be worn only with trousers.

T

TAN

So many cries of alarm have already been uttered by doctors and beauticians on the subject of suntans, that there is no need for me to add my own.

While a lightly suntanned complexion creates an agreeable impression of health, an overcooked epidermis is very aging and even in-elegant upon one's return to the city at the end of the summer. Is there a young woman who has not experienced the disappointment of discovering that the bronzed Adonis who was so divine on the beach or on the ski slopes has quite a different air when dressed in city clothes? In order to be attractive, a deep suntan requires the open air, very décolleté necklines, bare arms, and bright, clear colours (particularly blue, yellow, and white). The rather neutral shades of town apparel often make a suntanned bathing beauty look more like an anemic African.

Tanned legs stay brown for a very long time, and it is best to wear a definitely darker shade of nylon stockings after the summer vacation, because pale nylons seem white and opaque when worn over a dark skin.

The mania of returning from a holiday as deeply tanned as possible was perhaps understandable when the idea was to turn green with envy one's unfortunate friends who remained behind in the city all summer long. But nowadays, when everybody manages to get a fair share of the sun, I really do not see the point of wasting so much time baking oneself to a crisp.

The friends who have known me since my youth will say that I used to hold entirely different views. That is true. And that is also why you might as well profit from the experience of a woman who has hopelessly spoiled a perfectly normal complexion by too much sunbathing!

TEENAGERS

The young girls between thirteen and eighteen years of age who were completely ignored by the fashion industry not so long ago, have become one of the most important consumer groups in America – and the same phenomenon is occurring in certain European countries too. Instead of having to choose between the childish styles of the girls' department, which were obviously no longer suited to them, and the adult modes of the women's department, which were even less adapted to their age and figures, they now find entire floors devoted to teenage fashions in all the large department stores. Modern merchants, manufacturers, and designers, keenly aware of the economic importance of the younger clientele in countries where the population is steadily becoming rejuvenated, are only too willing to cater to the whims and fancies of their juvenile customers.

Fashion buyers and stylists take great pains to study the trends of teenage taste, and the college shops that are opened toward the end of the summer school holidays are often staffed entirely by teenagers. These shops are generously stocked with all the favourite campus fashions: plaid skirts and heavy sweaters, Bermuda shorts, long patterned wool socks, moccasins and blue jeans, as well as more short-lived modes such as suspenders, men's vests, low-waisted skirts and trousers, and baseball caps. At the same time, specialized magazines with a particularly young outlook, such as *Seventeen, Glamour,* and *Moe,* give excellent advice on fashion and beauty care to teenagers, teaching them how to care for their skin, how to dress their hair, how to select appropriate outfits and the correct accessories for sports, city, and evening wear.

The result of all these efforts is that what used to be known as 'the awkward age' has become one of the most charming periods of a woman's life. Since they have at last been given fashions of their own, today's teenagers are more satisfied to dress their age and less tempted by over-sophisticated styles.

Nevertheless, there are still a few absolute TABOOS for teenagers, which are not always sufficiently respected:

- earrings before 17 years of age.
- umbrellas before 15 years.
- real high heels before 16 years.

- nylon stockings (with the exception of bright-coloured tights) before 14 years.
- black (except for black velvet) before 18 years.
- draped dresses and necklines before 30 years.
- diamonds and all kinds of precious stones before 30 years . . . or until they are engaged to be married.

TRAVEL

If you consider that when you are far away from home and surrounded by strangers, you are judged entirely on the strength of your external appearance, perhaps you will realize the importance of being flawlessly well-dressed whenever you travel. Which means that your clothes should be perfectly adapted to your role of traveller and not give the impression that you are on your way to a wedding with a veiled hat and a fur stole – or, at the opposite extreme, toward the conquest of Annapurna with a knapsack on your back. On the excuse that travel so often leads to a holiday resort, there is a dismaying tendency today to set forth already dressed for that first sun bath. Campers may be forgiven this kind of nonchalance, since they can only carry on their backs a certain number of pounds. But if you are no longer a

Girl Scout, you must approach the problem from another angle.

In trains, planes, or cars, if you are traveling from one city to another, you should wear a city outfit. With this basic ensemble you will need really very little in your suitcase if your accessories have been carefully planned: In the winter – your black pumps, black purse, and coat will be just as appropriate for all your evening wear as for the means of locomotion you use. In the summer your bag and shoes might be beige; a lightweight coat and a dressier stole in a neutral colour will combine attractively with the two or three little dresses in your luggage.

During three seasons out of four, a suit is the mainstay of your wardrobe. It can be warmed up by a blouse or sweater or, it can be worn alone when the weather is mild. It is the ideal traveller; whether it is of wool, linen, or cotton, nothing else is as practical.

When travelling by car, you can be a bit more casual. A coat and matching skirt are ideal. All you need to add in summer is a lightweight dress in a colour that goes well with the coat, a blouse, and a sweater. With just these few basic elements you can cover a considerable amount of mileage and always be correctly attired.

If you are travelling from a city to a vacation resort, a suit is still your best outfit for traveling. You might wear with it: in the winter – a coat and warm boots; in the summer – a blouse or light sweater, with the indispensable lightweight coat over your arm.

Finally, if you are lucky enough to embark on a long sea voyage, there exists an established set of rules, which it is wise to respect: Arrive on board in a rather casual ensemble; never dress for dinner the first and last nights at sea, but deck yourself out in your best evening clothes on the other nights; relax in sports clothes during the morning; appear for lunch in a slightly less informal outfit. All of which necessitates a mountain of luggage, to the great joy of the few remaining women of unlimited wealth and leisure, who would rather travel by boat than any other way and thus enjoy one of the last orgies of luxury that have survived in our age of interplanetary rockets.

When you are going to visit a new country for the first time, it is a good idea to find out beforehand what is the customary manner of dress, so that you will not have to rush to the first shop you can find and buy an entirely new wardrobe, or stoically face the ordeal of being stared at like a Martian.

TROUSERS

Men must have singularly changed through the ages in order finally to accept the fact that women have as much right to wear pants as they, for it is one of their sacred privileges which they never have enjoyed sharing, even with Joan of Arc.

While it was the custom fifty years ago to dress little boys just like little girls, today little girls are dressed like boys. So it really isn't surprising that, after having passed half of their childhood in trousers, the girls wish to continue to wear them all the rest of their lives – even after they have acquired contours that are sometimes far too feminine to fit into man-tailored trousers.

Once you have experienced the comfort of trousers, it is difficult to wear anything else.

At home, the lounging pajamas so popular these past few years are being replaced by long hostess gowns, which are a thousand times more becoming and elegant.

𝒰

UNIFORMITY

Thanks to the high standard of living in the Occident and to the perfection of mass-produced Western fashions, an untrained observer must have the impression that every woman is dressed exactly alike.

I do not know the origin of this modern form of modesty, which has swept through the feminine population from San Francisco to Paris, and which seems to cause all women to want to resemble each other – even though at the same time they are spending more and more on their clothes, cosmetics, and hairdressers! I am however sure of one thing: this mass movement toward conformity will sooner or later oblige the high-fashion couturiers to turn to wholesale designing, even more inevitably because of the fantastic cost of custom-made clothes.

I must confess that I haven't the courage to go to

war against the famous little black dress that is the uniform of all our dinner parties. Besides, I realize that it can be extremely practical. But it should be considered one of the useful basic items of a minimum wardrobe, to be supplemented by other less stereotyped dressy ensembles, according to your means. And in any case, an elegant woman always attempts to relieve its banality by selecting a particularly refined design, or by placing a jewel in an original manner.

But if you really enjoy being dressed exactly like everybody else, then your future is rosy. Uniformity is a natural by-product of an automatized society, and – who knows? – perhaps one day individuality will be considered a crime.

In the meantime, you can always join the Army.

V

VEILS

Somewhat out of fashion at the moment (and I cannot imagine why), veils are one of the most flattering of feminine adornments. Perhaps the reason for their present lack of favour is that they became extremely widely adopted as a substitute for hats, which was an easy-to-wear mode, inexpensive, becoming, and practical! But since fashions are often no more than shooting stars, the brighter they shine, the quicker they expire.

A veil is always a dressy accessory, and except in the case of elderly ladies who can veil their faces from morning to night with great distinction, it is not really correct to wear a veil before 5 P.M. The size of the mesh should be selected in view of your particular personality type; a "femme fatale" can emphasize her seductive mystery with a rather heavy, coarse, veil, while the feminine ingenue should underline her charm with a fine misty froth of tulle. As far as colour is concerned, there are no restrictions – but black is almost always the most chic.

Let's hope that the designers will revive the mode of veils worn over the entire face and not only over the eyes. A full veil adds a lovely air of mystery and distinction to the most ordinary features, so that even the most humdrum housewife gives the impression of being on her way to some romantic rendezvous.

W

WATCHES

It is very difficult to find a really elegant wrist watch, even in the collections of the most famous jewellers. Either you must satisfy yourself with a plain man-style gold watch, square in shape and preferably mounted on a black suede watchband, which is smart with sports ensembles and whose very platitude is the source of its chic; or you can launch yourself in the costly purchase of a jeweled bracelet that conceals a watch beneath a simple decorative motif. However, aside from the fact that it is impossible to discreetly find out what time it is, the latter designs are seldom very refined.

At any rate, the tiny diamond wrist watch, which was the vogue before the war, has completely gone out of fashion.

Unless you are fortunate enough to own an

antique jeweled clip or pin in the shape of a flower or a bird which carries in its heart a tiny watch, like the masterpieces of Fabergé, it is better to resist the modern versions of these fanciful styles, for they are much less beautiful in design and workmanship than the originals. The fact is that a watch is above all a utilitarian object, and it can be more or less camouflaged only up to a certain point.

The last time I scoured the shops looking for a wrist watch that was attractive and out of the ordinary, I finally ended up by designing it myself; and since I still like it and wear it, I suppose that it can be considered a success. It is of gold, and so I only wear it during the day-time or to very informal dinners, in which case I can turn it upside down so that the watch face is concealed, and it then looks like an ordinary gold bracelet.

A final word of advice: Since a watch is essentially a practical day-time accessory, there is really no point in buying one that is very dressy and expensive.

WEATHER

Aside from being the number one subject of polite conversation all over the world, the weather is also a favorite excuse for lapses of elegance committed by women who are normally very careful about their appearance. And yet, being well dressed come rain or shine or snow does not necessarily mean being condemned to catch pneumonia every winter and to succumb to heat stroke when the temperature soars. Some of the most attractive national outfits in the world have been created in countries where the climate is extreme, like the cool and graceful Indian sari, or the romantic outfit of the Russian Cossacks; and within the limits of occidental elegance, there are a number of ways in which a well-dressed woman can adapt her attire to the rigors of a Siberian cold wave or a tropical month of August.

During extremely cold weather, she can:

 - keep warm by wearing a thin, close-fitting silk undershirt (with a low-cut neckline and short sleeves or none at all so that it will not show) instead of piling sweaters and cardigans on top of a pretty wool dress, which is certain to destroy its chic.
 - wear long stretch tights instead of sheer nylon stockings (bright-coloured tights in the country, and stocking-coloured ones with a city ensemble).

- dress like a ski champion or a Canadian trapper in the
  country if she wishes, but never, never wear ski pants
  on a city street.
- wear long evening gowns instead of short ones whenever possible, and at-home outfits consisting of a long
  wool skirt and long-sleeved jersey or sweater tops.
- take advantage of stoles, which can add a great deal of
  elegance and warmth to suits, daytime and evening
  dresses, and even coats, if they are made of the same
  material. Silk evening stoles can be interlined with
  flannel for added insulation over low-cut gowns.

When the mercury moves in the opposite direction,
the problem becomes somewhat more difficult, because there is a limit to the amount of clothing that a
woman can decently remove. Nevertheless,

During a tropical heat wave she can:

- simplify her undergarments by reducing them to the
  least possible number of separate pieces.
- remember that cotton lingerie is much cooler than
  nylon, and that a lined skirt is cooler than a separate
  slip, which has the added disadvantage (especially
  nylon slips) of clinging to the legs.

- wear sleeveless linen, cotton, or silk dresses with scooped-out necklines, but never display a deep décolleté or a bare back in the city.
- prefer pale colours, which are psychologically cooler than dark or vivid shades.
- realize that flared and pleated skirts are more comfortable than straight ones, and also less apt to crease.
- avoid belted waistlines in favor of trapeze and Empire styles, which allow the air to circulate around the waist.
- remember that open sandals are never elegant in the city in the daytime, and that rubber or synthetic soles are unbearable during hot weather; low-cut pumps are the smartest solution, but sling-back pumps, open at the heels, are also permissible.
- realize that stockings are actually an aid to foot comfort in the summer heat; if, however, the custom in your city or office is to go bare-legged during the hottest months of the year, you should first make sure that your legs are nicely sun-tanned and perfectly groomed.
- whenever possible, wear a straw hat, which always has a refreshing effect, particularly if the brim is wide enough to cast a cool shadow on your face and the back of your neck.

– adopt a lighter scent than the one used during the winter, and prefer eau de cologne and eau de toilette to more concentrated perfume.

– follow the example of the British in the tropics: cover your head whenever you go out of doors, change your clothes as often as possible, bathe frequently, and always walk on the shady side of the street!

(See Rain)

WEDDINGS

A bride-to-be never dreams of getting married in her everyday clothes, even for the most informal ceremony. If circumstances or her financial means do not permit her to wear the traditional white wedding gown, she wishes at least to appear in something new on that happy occasion. Her best solution in this case is to buy a smart suit and a very pretty hat, which can be of any style at all except for a flowered or white feather headdress with a veil.

Nothing strikes me as more pathetic than to see on Saturday morning at the doors of a church some young bride who could only afford half of a wedding ensemble, when it would have been much more charming and easier on her budget too if she had simply selected a normal city outfit. The same is true for members of the wedding party, who also have every interest in avoiding chi-chis and pastel shades which will be of no use to them later on. I am not particularly fond of informal short white wedding dresses, and it seems to me that if you haven't the desire or the means to invest in the complete outfit, it is preferable to abandon it completely.

A long, formal wedding dress is elegant only when it is utterly simple, even somewhat austere. Only the material in which it is made should be sumptuous – heavy lace or very heavy mat satin. Of course, the season, the importance of the wedding, and the bride's personal type influence the choice a great deal.

Tall, thin brides will find it advantageous to accentuate their sculptural beauty by dressing in a sheath of heavy material with a *manteau de cour* – a sort of cape attached to the shoulders – which forms a train; long sleeves; and a simple diadem in their hair. Small, very young brides would do better to place the accent on their doll-like charm by wearing a wedding dress of tulle, lace, or organdy in the summer, with a full puffed skirt, no train, little short sleeves, short white gloves, and a headdress or bonnet which adds to their height.

The veil becomes somewhat of a problem when wedding photographs are taken on the church steps after the ceremony, because many of them are lovely when they hang down in front of the face, but much less so after they have been thrown back to form a huge and often somewhat lopsided halo. As a general rule, I am not in favor of utilizing the family heirloom lace veil that has been passed down from mother to daughter for generations. Even though it may be worth a fortune, I have found that not only does it add nothing to a modern wedding dress, but it usually destroys its elegance completely.

Beware also of too heavy trains which cling to the carpet and make the young bridal couple resemble (unfortunate image!) a couple of convicts dragging a ball and chain.

To accompany these long, formal wedding gowns, the bridegroom should obligatorily wear a morning coat, as should all the other male members of the wedding party. It is no longer fashionable for the women members of the family to wear long dresses. The most elegant ensemble at any season is certainly a silk coat worn over a matching dress. Even

Great-grandmother should not wear black on this occasion, but softer tones such as prune, grey, beige, or pale blue-grey.

For a mother of the bride who has a perfect figure (and don't most modern mothers look just as young as their daughters?), a silk suit or a dress-and-jacket ensemble is also an excellent solution. The hat in all cases can be rather large, of either wool or velvet in the winter, and straw in the summer. For grandmothers in every season a little hat of tulle or veiling is most becoming and can form a very soft and elegant colour scheme if it is of a different shade of the same colour as the ensemble.

You can also match your shoes and gloves to your outfit and have a little flat purse made out of the same material; but it is better not to have every single element of your ensemble in exactly the same shade. If you are extremely refined, you might plan on carrying an extra pair of gloves in your purse, especially if they are white or pale ones, because they will probably no longer look fresh after they have gone through the ordeal of the receiving line following the wedding ceremony.

The bride's attendants at the most elegant modern weddings are usually little children. My own favorite formula is: nothing but little boys dressed like choir-boys with a long red robe, red slippers, and a white surplice – although it is necessary for them to change their clothes before the reception, since this outfit may only be worn inside a church.

Little girl attendants are also very charming, and they are always absolutely thrilled to wear a long, romantic dress, a little bonnet, very short gloves, and to carry a tiny bouquet. The material for these dresses should be very simple, such as cotton piqué. They can be accompanied by Little Lord Fauntleroys wearing long trousers, ruffled shirts, and wide fringed satin sashes.

The colours should of course be the same for the little boys and the little girls. The best scheme is: white dresses, with the bonnets, sashes, and bouquets of the same colour; and for the boys, black velvet or white satin trousers, white satin shirts, and sashes the same colour as those worn by the little girls.

In France, the newlyweds disappear as discreetly as possible during the reception. But in the Anglo-Saxon countries, all the wedding guests gather round to see them off on their wedding trip. This is the moment to appear in an extremely elegant traveling outfit: in summer, a white linen suit worn with a dark blouse, dark gloves, hat and shoes; and in winter, a tweed suit or dress under a coat. The bride should leave the reception in this ensemble even if the actual honeymoon departure isn't scheduled until the next day and if, as soon as she is out of sight, she removes her hat, gloves and shoes – which are certainly her only enemies on that particular day.

It is no longer unusual for a woman to be married more than once. The more advanced one's age, the more restricted should be the number of guests invited to attend the wedding ceremony – which in this case is merely a formality establishing a change of civil status. An elegant ensemble, such as you might wear to a smart luncheon – a suit or wool coat and dress, and a simple hat – seems to me the most appropriate outfit, in any colour you like including black, but never under any circumstances white.

WEEKENDS

After five days of gradual asphyxiation in town, an ever increasing number of city dwellers escape to the country for the weekend to fill their lungs with forty-eight hours' worth of fresh air. As a result, an entire industry has been built around this desire for pastoral leisure, and never before have so many sports clothes been sold.

The ideal outfit for an elegant woman who is leaving to spend the weekend in the country with friends consists of:

- a suit, worn with flat-heeled shoes (or boots in the winter), and a handsome handbag of the traveling type.

In the winter, spring, and autumn, the suit would be made of rather heavy tweed in blended tones and worn with a harmonizing sweater, and it would be covered either by a waterproof coat or a sporty coat. In the summer, the suit material would be a bright-coloured linen or cotton, and it would be accompanied by a shirtwaist, sandals, and a straw handbag. Her overnight bag should contain:

- a simple dressing gown that is neither sheer nor voluminous, but pretty and fresh-looking for breakfast, which everybody will probably take together in the dining room.
- a pair of trousers, a sweater or blouse, and, in the summer.

- a bathing suit and a sundress.
- for the evening: a trouser suit if the evening is to be spent informally at home with her friends; or
- a long dinner dress, slightly décolleté, if her weekend hostess leads a more formal kind of life, or if there is to be a dinner party on Saturday night; but if the weekend program includes an informal cocktail-buffet type of evening, a more appropriate outfit would be:
- in the winter: a very simple white jersey dress with a bateau neckline, or a sleeveless wool sheath in a pale colour; and in the summer: a dress of the same type in printed cotton or linen.

If she is invited to participate in any kind of active sport, she should remember to bring all of the appropriate attire. Nothing is more annoying for a weekend hostess than to have to appear at the club with a badly dressed friend, or else to be obliged to lend a white tennis skirt, riding boots, or merely a pair of sensible walking shoes to the improvident guest whose only footwear is spike-heeled pumps that wouldn't last much further than the front doorstep.

In short, even if you are not at all an outdoor type

of woman at heart, you should at least dress the part when you spend the weekend in the country, and by all means leave your false eyelashes in town.

X

XMAS

Christmas is a very special occasion. You prepare for it weeks ahead of time, thinking mostly of others and of the pleasure you hope to give them. If there is one time during the year when you ought to feel good, affectionate, kind-hearted, thoughtful, and generous, it is certainly at Christmas.

It is only natural to harmonize your physical appearance with these beautiful moral qualities, and this for the average woman means a new dress, a lovely hairdo, and perhaps a beauty treatment. Besides, it is also a means of honouring the gift you are sure to receive – because deep down in your heart, you expect your kind-heartedness, thoughtfulness, generosity, etc. (see above) to be rewarded, and in large measure too – for instance, a piece of jewellery in exchange for a necktie!

According to the type of Christmas party you may be invited to attend, the ideal outfit is a long or short evening dress, and, without going so far as to try to outsparkle the Christmas tree, it is perfectly appropriate for you to make a special effort to create a splendid appearance.

If you are spending Christmas in the country or in the mountains, or if your Christmas eve is to be a quiet evening at home or *à deux*, a hostess gown or velvet lounging pajamas brightened up with outfit jewellery would be just right – unless you prefer a short, embroidered felt or wool skirt worn with bright-coloured tights and a low-cut sweater top.

The point to remember is that this is a very special evening, and it merits the honour of a very special manner of dress.

Y

YACHTING

The only thing that should float in the wind on board a yacht are the ship's colours. A dress or skirt that does the same would be quite out of place. Consequently, a simple, even slightly masculine style of clothing is more advisable. Besides, pleasure boats are not usually equipped with generous closets capable of containing a lot of complicated dresses.

If you are lucky enough to be cruising in warm waters, you will need:

– several quick-drying bathing suits (the backbone of
  your wardrobe).
– a terry-cloth bathrobe.
– shorts and a cotton top for luncheon aboard, which is
  the most torrid moment of the day.

- a real beach dress.
- a linen skirt or trousers and a blouse, for lunching ashore.
- woollen garments for the cool of evening, and finally;
- a slightly dressier dress for dining ashore in a smart restaurant.

If you are cruising in a colder climate, you will need several heavy sweaters, a good coat, wool socks, and a linen suit for shore excursions. The general custom on board some sailing yachts is to go barefoot all day long; on others, the skipper prefers his crew and guests to wear non-skid trainers. Aside from these, you will need several pairs of sandals or espadrilles to wear ashore, but never in any case heels of any kind, which ruin the deck.

The visored admiral's cap should be avoided like the plague. An old linen hat is your smartest protection from the blazing sun, and solid-coloured cotton or chiffon scarves from the wind.

Now is your chance to show everyone that you are not afraid to be seen without make-up, that you never leave a trail of disorder in your wake, that you have a wonderfully even disposition, and that your elegance is based on utter simplicity. If this be the case (and if you are not subject to seasickness and know how to swim), you will surely have the most wonderful time of your life.

ZIPPERS

Zippers must have been invented by some weary and impatient husband, tired of the nightly ritual of unfastening an endless row of tiny buttons running down the back of his wife's dress! Whatever their source of inspiration, zippers are a marvellous technical development, but unfortunately less admirable from an aesthetic point of view. They should therefore be as imperceptible as possible, dyed to match the garment, concealed in a flat-lying placket, and no longer than is necessary to permit getting into and out of a garment with ease.

The most serious defect of zippers is their lack of suppleness. Ideal where a smooth, straight line is desired, they cannot be used in a dress that is bloused or draped, and should be replaced in this case by alternating hooks-and-eyes and snap fasteners, or by alternating buttons and hooks-and-eyes. A back closed by buttons is undeniably more chic than a zipper, but it is far more troublesome. Most couturiers dislike zipper closings on long sleeves too, but here again, zippers are so much more practical than buttons!

Considerate designers try to avoid placing a zipper where it can cause discomfort – where you might have to sit on it, for example – as well as where the extra fraction of an inch added by the zipper placket would thicken the waist or hipline. For this reason, back zippers are preferred for dresses, front zippers – just like a man's – for trousers, and two short zippers at each side of the back for straight skirts.

ZOOLOGY

Making a public appearance with a baby panther, a tame crocodile, or an orangutan, even a very intelligent one, should be reserved for starlets in need of publicity, for it creates a circus atmosphere that is quite incompatible with the discreet behaviour of an elegant woman. However, the situation is quite different if one's animal companion is our most faithful of friends, the dog.

Ever since antiquity it has been considered elegant to own a dog, and some of the most beautiful women in history have taken great pains to make sure that they would leave this earthly existence accompanied by their favorite pet. Even though you may look awful, be badly dressed, tired, sick of everything and everybody, and feel utterly neglected, you will always find in your dog's limpid eyes unlimited admiration and unconditional fidelity. Sometimes I think that dogs must have been created especially in order to improve our morale and to give us a good opinion of ourselves when we are most in need of encouragement.

In return for these inestimable gifts, they demand of the city dweller mindful of her elegance a minimum of effort and organization. London is undoubtedly the city in which there is the greatest number of women with the most perfect understanding of the problems posed by the possession, grooming, exercising – in short, by the happy cohabitation of a woman and a dog. When walking their pets in Hyde Park or around a tree-lined Georgian square, these English ladies always wear comfortable, low-heeled shoes and suits in a hazy blend of colours on which an affectionate but muddy paw will leave no indelible trace.

If you own a real doggy dog, who loves to jump and play, you might as well banish from your wardrobe white or pastel coats and skirts. If your dog belongs to one of the long-haired breeds, you should beware of certain synthetic fabrics that attract his shedding coat like a magnet. You would also do well to avoid all of the very loosely woven fabrics which consist of countless tiny traps for a puppy's claw.

There are certain lap dogs like the Papillon, Yorkshire Terrier, Chihauhua, Pekingese, and the miniature Schnauzer, that pose no problem at all since they usually move from their owner's car to a well-heated living room, very often without placing a paw on the ground.

Alas, it must be recognized that there is a fashion in dogs, and a breed which was the rage during a number of years, like the Airedale or the Wire-haired and Smooth-haired Fox Terrier, mysteriously disappears one day simply because it has ceased to be in vogue, just like an old hat. There are even certain breeds, disdainfully referred to in Europe as *chiens de concierge* (janitor's dogs), in whose company an elegant woman would no longer care to be seen, such as the Pomeranian and the Fox Terrier, which are nevertheless among the most intelligent of all. At the same time, any kind of a miniature Poodle, more or less bleached, or any Dachshund with long, short or wiry hair, has the right to tear apart the cushions of the most aristocratic houses in Paris. There are even certain breeds that are appreciated almost exclusively by royal families, like the Welsh Corgis of the Queen of England, the Pug dogs of the Windsors, and the English Bulldogs which nowadays are seen mainly in a few ducal palaces.

Whatever his breed – and even if he is a unique specimen of unknown origin – your dog deserves to be as well-groomed as his mistress. A few minutes a day devoted to brushing and combing, inspecting the ears and paws, and wiping his eyes, can do wonders for his appearance and self-esteem. Don't forget to ask your veterinary to clean his teeth and clip his claws from time to time, and whenever necessary, treat him to a bath even if he howls with rage. Breeds like the Poodle and Wire-haired Fox Terrier should have their coats clipped regularly, and this is best performed by a specialist unless you are very expert, because canine haircuts must comply with the official Kennel Club standards if you wish your dog to be admired and eligible for show.

In many cities there are canine couturiers, but in

this field as in so many others, eccentricity should be avoided. Collars studded with rhinestones, for example, are rather vulgar. It is preferable to select a collar and leash of a colour that is becoming to your dog's coat, or even plain black, limiting its ornamentation to gilt studs at the very most; and for the winter, a matching coat.

Acknowledgements

As a closing word, I would like to express my gratitude to all those who have helped me in the preparation of this book with their advice or their personal example of elegance:

Madame Hervé Alphand
Madame Hélène Arpels
Mrs David Bruce
Mr John Fairchild
Comtesse de Gramont
Wladimir de Kousmine
Mrs Raymond Loewy
Madame de Miraval
Vicomtesse de Ribes
Mr Robert Ricci

Comtesse de Roquemaurel
Mr Percival Savage
Madame Nicole de Vesian

and especially Madame Georges Lillaz, whose elegance
of heart matches her elegance of appearance.

GENEVIEVE ANTOINE DARIAUX